# SECRET
# MOBILE

## A Guide to the Weird, Wonderful, and Obscure

Amy Delcambre

Library of Congress Control Number: 2022937096
ISBN: 9781681064048

Design by Jill Halpin
All photos are courtesy of the author or believed to be in the public domain unless otherwise noted.

Printed in the United States of America
22 23 24 25 26  5 4 3 2 1

For Lillianne, Eilie, and Lucia, my three beautiful adventures, who keep me curious, wild, and weird, and for Sean and Jude for watching over us and for reminding me that life is a brief and precious gift in a world that begs to be experienced.

"You only live once, but if you do it right, once is enough."
—Mae West

"When all else fails, throw a party!"
—Eugene Walter

# CONTENTS

# ACKNOWLEDGMENTS

Writing a book about a city that's over 300 years old takes a village. I couldn't have succeeded without the following people's knowledge, conversation, and encouragement.

Thank you to Erwin Craighead, Michael Thomason, Jay Higginbottom, Caldwell Delaney, Joe Cuhaj, Elizabeth Parker, Susan Rouillier, Frye Gaillard, and Malcom Steiner, writers whose documentaries were vital jigsaw pieces to this telling of Mobile's story. Thank you to Carolyn Haines, Frye Gaillard, and Thomas Lakeman, my university writing professors who have remained supportive friends and colleagues and whose genius and passion continue to inspire me.

Thank you to the editors and publishers—Rob Holbert (the *Lagniappe*), Ed Moore, and Gary Ellis (Compass Media), and Laura Holloway (The Storyteller Agency) for writing opportunities and skills without which this book wouldn't be possible.

Thank you to Angela Trigg (Haunted Bookshop), Chuck Torries (Mobile History Museum), Cart Blackwell (Mobile Carnival Museum), Tom McGhee (Bellingrath Gardens and Home), Ben Raines (America's Amazon Adventures), and Jeanne Jones (McCall Library) for leads and interviews.

Thank you to Amanda Doyle, Barbara Northcott, Chelcie Grant, and everyone at Reedy Press for your support in helping me produce this incredible collection of quirky history.

Thank you to my parents for a lifetime of stories about Mobile and for raising me to believe there's nothing I can't do.

Thank you to my late husband, Sean, for believing in me, for loving me unconditionally, and for helping me launch Traveling with Stories. Your love and faith are eternal gifts and motivators.

Thank you to my amazing partner and dear friend, Bucky Hicks. Your support and love are almost as incredible as your wealth of arcane knowledge about Mobile. Thank you for sharing your stories.

Above all, thank you to my girls, who inspire me to do crazy, wonderful things . . . like write books.

# INTRODUCTION

Was Mobile really the site of the first Mardi Gras? Who is Joe Cain? How do they make the gardens grow at Bellingrath? Was the city's founder really covered in tattoos? Are there really manatees in Mobile Bay? Why are there bees on the roof of a hotel downtown?

I spent my life in Mobile and took for granted that Joe Cain Day was integral to Mardi Gras—didn't everyone celebrate that? It wasn't until I did some digging that I learned the real history behind the traditions that surround Carnival and the story of Mobile.

Mobile is a city of celebration and history—often these things are richly intertwined, but rarely do we dive beneath the surface to understand the why of our weird, wonderful, wild city. In digging deep to unearth Mobile's secrets, I learned we're a port city founded on rebellion, innovation, debauchery, piety, generosity, and hospitality. That's where I'm taking you in *Secret Mobile*.

This book is a travel and local interest guide. It's designed to help locals delve into the quirky connections and the vast history that define Mobile's character and story.

To discover these secrets for this rich tapestry of stories, I consulted books, photos, historians, storytellers, writers, curators, artists, locals, documentaries, family, friends, and personal experience.

I looked for a range of oddities that reveal the hidden treasures in the natural and man-made institutions that Mobile comprises. I featured stories and characters that connected to local businesses and activities—*Secret Mobile* is more than a book of stories; it's an immersive experience.

As you'll see, in Mobile, there's always more to the story, and usually there's more than one side to the story, too. Share your secret stories and experiences on Instagram and Facebook with #SecretMobileAl, and let's discover Mobile's secrets together!

# MASSACRE ISLAND

## Why was Dauphin Island once called Massacre Island?

. . . And should we be afraid? The name Massacre Island does have a lot more street cred, if you will, than Dauphin Island. One can only assume that pirates would've thought twice before attempting to pillage a place called Massacre Island, though that's not the reason for either of the names given to Mobile's treasured barrier island.

Pierre Le Moyne Sieur d'Iberville landed on the island in 1699. Upon anchoring, he discovered a large pile of bones and skulls, the flesh not fully rotted off. Naturally, he assumed the worst and, given that Google wouldn't exist for quite some time, he had no way of knowing that the massacre site was actually a Mississippian burial mound exposed by a hurricane that had recently blown through (there was no Weather Channel either).

The name was changed in 1707 to Dauphin Island by d'Iberville to honor the Dauphin de France, Louis XV, who would one day ascend the throne. Often, the name is confused as *Dolphin* Island in honor of the docile mammals that dwell in Gulf waters. This may be in part due to the fact that Mobilians largely pronounce *Dauphin* as *dolphin*.

The Indian shell mounds, which are land formations composed of oyster shells from when the Native Americans ate seafood on the island, are considered a sacred space, and some suggest they're haunted by the spirits of those who remain there. Some claim to hear echoing beats, like drums, at

Evidence from a 1975 archeological dig suggests a prehistoric settlement from the Bayou La Batre-Tchefuncte culture at Indian Shell Mound Park 4,500 to 3,200 years ago.

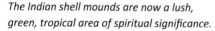

*The Indian shell mounds are now a lush, green, tropical area of spiritual significance.*

night, while others say they see white lights, which are possibly spirits glowing from the shells. Call it what you want, but local indigenous tribes do say there's an ancestral connection at this site, which is why visitors should be respectful and reverent.

## INDIAN SHELL MOUND PARK

**What:** Park and birding refuge where piles of shells were found

**Where:** 830 Desoto Dr., Dauphin Island

**Cost:** Free

**Pro Tip:** Visit the trail mound site at 2 N Iberville Dr. You'll find a shell ring among other features.

# THE SERPENTS OF BIENVILLE

### Did Mobile's founding father really have tattoos?

Somehow, when writing history, biographers left out the fine detail about Bienville having tattoos. Jean-Baptiste Le Moyne de Bienville, the younger and less experienced of the two Le Moyne brothers, was charged with literally holding down the fort at 27 Mile Bluff, the original Mobile settlement.

The settlement comprised a motley crew of Creoles, Native Americans from differing tribes (many Mauvillas or Mobile Indians who'd been relatively destroyed by Spanish explorer Hernando de Soto over a century prior), African Americans, and French. It was allegedly mutually beneficial that these splinter groups make nice. For the Mauvillas, alliance with Bienville would afford protection against the Creek and Alabama tribes; for Bienville, it would mean protection, sustenance, and education on how to thrive in this new land.

In a show of solidarity and as a means to solidify trust, Bienville submitted himself for heavy tattooing. Henri de Tonti writes of a large Constantinian cross inked into Bienville's stomach as well as a large winding serpent that writhed around Bienville's body with a tongue that gestured toward Bienville's nether regions.

Bienville reportedly wore nothing or a cloth, the same fashion as the Native Americans, during their visits, his tattoos,

---

The original 27 Mile Bluff settlement was abandoned because of flooding caused by a hurricane. In 1711, it was relocated to where Fort Condé now stands at Mobile Bay.

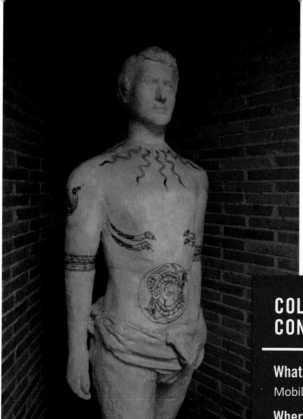

*The tattooed statue of Bienville at the Fort Condé site reveals that Bienville's tattoos made him fearsome to his enemies in battle.*

## COLONIAL FORT CONDÉ MUSEUM

**What:** Battery where the City of Mobile was settled in 1711

**Where:** 150 S Royal St.

**Cost:** $5–$10

**Pro Tip:** Fully immerse yourself in history by staying at the AAA four-diamond historic Fort Condé Inn.

which were received through a painful process involving a needle or sharp bone opening the skin and filled with a colored powder, fully visible.

As the South became increasingly conservative due to English Puritan influence and influxes of conservatives during the 1900s, the story of the city's founder's tattoos became arcane. As of 2013, though, a revitalized exhibit at Fort Condé displays a statue of Bienville with a few tattoos on his torso; though, many accounts suggest that Bienville's flesh was fully covered with snakes and that his tattoos gave him a high degree of credibility among his Native American colleagues.

# THE MAN WITH THE IRON HAND

## What does the hook-handed Father of Arkansas have to do with Mobile?

Mobile was initially "discovered" by the French (the Native Americans who already lived here not withstanding), but Henri de Tonti was an Italian expatriate who'd made his way to the burgeoning colonies in the 1600s with René Robert Cavelier, Sieur de La Salle.

In his early explorations along the Illinois and Mississippi Rivers, de Tonti established St. Louis and a post on the Arkansas River, which would eventually become the state of Arkansas . . . though, de Tonti's settlement in Arkansas would not be further developed until the 1700s after his death (not to spoil the story) and the settlement of Mobile.

Speaking of Mobile, what does the man dubbed the Father of Arkansas have to do with Mobile? Pierre Le Moyne d'Iberville set sail for Mobile in 1699. Upon arriving in Mobile Bay, he ascended a tree in search of the elusive Mississippi River, the purpose of his quest. He moved farther westward and established a fort at Biloxi.

It was around this time that he made the acquaintance of de Tonti, who assured d'Iberville that the river he was searching for existed. De Tonti joined d'Iberville's exploration, desperate to have his own claim to fame, to settle a colony.

---

When de Tonti was a boy, his hand was blown off by a grenade in the war against Spain. His replacement iron hook–hand earned him the nickname "Iron Hand."

*Iron Hand Brewing is named for the roguish de Tonti. The brewery serves British, German, and American dishes.*

He recalled his earlier exploration of Mobile Bay and the land barrier provided by "Massacre Island" (Dauphin Island). De Tonti looked for a space in the bay for the settlement. Twenty-seven miles north, he discovered a small band of Native Americans, remnants of the Tuscaloosa tribe, called the Mobilians. This would become Fort Louise de la Louisiane, the fort that d'Iberville would colloquially call Mobile.

De Tonti continued aiding the settlement by attempting to bridge peace between the Choctaw and Cherokee tribes and the French; he was instrumental to Bienville, so it was a blow when he died in 1704 from yellow fever.

## IRON HAND BREWING

**What:** Local brewery and eatery in the historic De Tonti district

**Where:** 206 State St.

**Cost:** Average $5 for a drink

**Pro Tip:** History buffs should pop into the brewery on a Monday night for the Mobile Civil War Roundtable group chat; local history authors and others attend.

# FLIGHT OF THE PELICAN GIRLS

## Why were French women shipped to Mobile?

In 1702, the French arrived in Mobile to "settle" the "New World." The original Fort Louis de la Louisiane was settled at 27 Mile Bluff located 27 miles north of modern Mobile. The younger of the brothers in charge, Jean-Baptiste Le Moyne de Bienville, was put in charge of the bluff, bless his heart.

The settlers pursued Native American women. To curtail this foolishness and to keep them busy on the very urgent business of settling, Bienville requested brides for his men from France. King Louis XIV sent orphaned virgins of "marrying age" (14–19) to the colony to wed the men and populate the colony.

The women were selected with some care as a similar project in Martinique had turned out disastrously (these women were volunteers of "questionable society," so that may have had something to do with it). In all, 23 young ladies arrived as un-besmirched as the leadership on board the *Le Pelican* could be expected to allow.

Upon arrival, the French women were besieged by many challenges, the first being yellow fever. A stop in Havana en route resulted in one young lady, Louise Francoise LeFevre, dying a day after she arrived. The rest, barring Gabrielle Bonet, who went insane upon being abandoned by her husband the morning after her wedding night, made matches.

---

### COLONIAL FORT CONDÉ

**What:** The location where 27 Mile Bluff was relocated in 1711

**Where:** 150 S Royal St.

**Cost:** $5–$10

**Pro Tip:** Refuel your tour with lunch at the Bistro St. Emanuel restaurant at Fort Condé Inn.

*A modern-day Joe Cain Marching Society group honors the Pelican Girls each year by donning period attire and parading the streets of downtown Mobile. Photo courtesy of Mike Dumas*

Problematically, however, the Frenchmen weren't keen on farming or building things (lovers, not fighters . . . got it), and the Pelican Girls who didn't eventually wipe out from yellow fever had to survive on acorns. They enacted the Petticoat Rebellion, denying their husbands bed and board until they had proper homes. Bienville derided them as spoiled but, to be fair, they didn't voluntarily leave Versailles for such foolishness.

Another name for Pelican Girls is "Casquette Girl" because the women who came to wed French colonists arrived only with a little case of their belongings (oh, and yellow fever).

# IF YOU GUMBO, YOU GUMBO

## How did gumbo find its way to the US?

Gumbo is an iconic Southern dish composed of a roux (a thick base), some kind of meat (chicken with sausage and shrimp with chicken are two combinations often seen), the Southern holy trinity (onions, peppers, celery), okra, and seasoning (bay leaves, garlic, etc.). Almost anything can go into a gumbo . . . but gumbo isn't gumbo until you have a dark, thick roux (otherwise, it's just soup), which is what Madame Langlois was making in the early 1700s. Here's what happened.

The Pelican Girls arrived to Fort Louis in 1704. Bienville, the Le Moyne brother in charge of the Mobile settlement, had his housekeeper, Madame Langlois, prepare a fish stew for the girls, which they adored. Madame had learned to cook available produce from the Native American tribes.

The Pelican Girls adored the stew. They added in the okra they'd obtained from enslaved Africans during their stop in the West Indies. The revised dish earned the moniker "gumbo" because the word okra is derivative of the African word for okra, *guingombo*. The addition of okra thickened the stew, and that's why we now assert that for gumbo to be gumbo, it has to be thick.

Thus, it was by way of Africa that okra arrived in the West Indies and eventually the US. The French slave trade, dating

## MUDBUGS

**What:** Fresh family-owned seafood market and counter-serve eatery

**Where:** 2005 Government St.

**Cost:** $7.99 for a bowl of gumbo, $3.99 for a side of okra

**Pro Tip:** Mudbugs is the place to go for fresh seafood to make your own gumbo . . . or try theirs . . . it's out of this world!

*Cooking okra can be tricky. Once heated, the vegetable gets "slimy." It takes skilled hands to make crispy fried okra.*

back to the 1600s, made okra's introduction to the West Indies, and the Pelican Girls brought it from there.

Unsurprisingly, gumbo is still heavily tied to the rich heritage of Creoles and African Americans in Mobile and to the African American Mardi Gras tradition. Gumbo is a savory experience in culture and in history, and the dish graces many a Mobile restaurant menu. It's worthwhile to try every preparation you find because no two family or restaurant gumbos are the same.

In 1940, after the first Mobile Area Mardi Gras Association (MAMGA) parade, the king and queen went to J. A. Franklin's home for gumbo and a champagne toast.

# PARK PLACE

## What's left of Mobile's "Coney Island"?

Today's Cooper Riverside Park, with the convention center, the cruise terminal, the GulfQuest National Maritime Museum of the Gulf of Mexico, and the *Perdido Queen* dinner cruise line, is a frail echo of the glorious waterfront of yesteryear. In the 1890s, the Bay Shell Road ran adjacent to the entirety of the Mobile Bay coastline, and everything was downtown.

Monroe Park was a veritable Coney Island. Constructed in the 1890s, the park featured a roller coaster, a carousel, the Wonderland Theater, a zoo, and other amusements designed to entice weekend tourism. Later came a baseball park where Babe Ruth smashed a home run. Farther down, the Crystal Pool was built out of an artisanal spring.

Continue down the road and you end up at Arlington Park, where they had the fairgrounds and horse racing. Arlington Point was a peninsula that extended into the bay and included a movie theater, a rock garden, and the Buccaneer Yacht Clubhouse.

Looking at the waterfront now, which is scarcely visible, it's hard to imagine *this* Mobile. It's even harder to imagine that a Mobilian in Monroe Park almost became the first in flight. John Fowler had all the right ideas for a plane, but he couldn't quite get it to work. The Wright brothers, though, did allegedly get a good look at his flying contraption in 1900 and used some of his concepts in their designs.

Fowler never flew, and hurricanes, war, financial stress, and westward expansion eventually moved everything away from

## MCNALLY PARK AND BOAT LAUNCH

**What:** Waterfront park on Bayfront Road

**Where:** 4380 Park Rd.

**Cost:** Free

**Pro Tip:** Walk down to the jetty at the boat launch and try to envision what Mobile's waterfront looked like 100 years ago.

*The Buccaneer Yacht Club is a private, member-only yacht and sailing club originally at Arlington Pier.*

the bustling waterfront. By 1946, Monroe Park ceased to exist, and Bay Shell Road had been broken up by new industry, including the airport, Brookley Field.

While the continuous road doesn't exist, you can still access Bay Front Road and ride along Mobile Bay. The water may not be accessible from downtown, but farther west you'll still find water.

Bay Shell Road was once the "most famous of all Alabama driveways." It was a six-mile stretch that ran from Choctaw Point to Brookley; the road closed in 1938.

# PRETTY IN PINK

### How did Mobile become Azalea City?

Mobile is a city of many monikers, one of which is "Azalea City," which is interesting since azaleas are indigenous to China. Perhaps even more interesting is that Mobile's azaleas provide a direct connection to our French founders.

French colonist Fifise Langlois paid a visit to his home in Toulouse, France, and, while he was there, harvested an azalea bush from his father's garden. He brought the plant back with him to Mobile in 1754 and planted it. The azalea proliferated and quickly became an object of notoriety and a tourism draw for Mobile.

Azaleas are woody plants that root heartily. Their delicate blooms typically only blossom a handful of times each year during spring after a cold spell. Their leaves remain evergreen, which makes them a popular and beautiful addition. The sight of a row of azaleas in bloom is breathtaking.

## MOBILE AZALEA TRAIL FESTIVAL

**What:** Events surrounding Azalea City during the last two weeks of March

**Where:** 111 S. Royal St.

**Cost:** Varies by event

**Pro Tip:** Take a ride down Springhill Avenue while the azaleas are in bloom; this was part of the original Azalea Trail.

It was this awareness that inspired local businessman Sam Lackland to encourage Mobilians to plant azaleas along city streets in 1929. The result was Mobile's famous Azalea Trail, which became a tourism draw throughout the 1940s. From its inception, the trail was officially opened each year by the Azalea Trail Maids.

The Azalea Trail Maids are city ambassadors who represent Mobile locally and nationally; in the mid-'50s, the program was so popular that girls from throughout Alabama and even outside of the state wanted to participate.

*Two Azalea Trail Maids from the 2021–2022 court greet athletes and spectators at the 2022 Azalea Trail Run.*

The Azalea Trail Maid program grew too large and was revised to permit only 50 Mobile County high school seniors; however, an out-of-state program, America's Junior Miss, was launched to accommodate other ambitious young scholars. The once-televised competition brings a distinguished winner from each state coming to Mobile each year to compete for the title of America's Junior Miss.

Their period attire—antebellum-style dresses— has caused ruffles in recent years; however, the pastel-colored dresses are arguably intended to symbolize flowers more than antiquity.

# BURN, BABY, BURN

## Who started Mobile's biggest fire in the 1800s?

Once upon a time—specifically the 1830s—Mobile was a rapidly growing metro area. The booming cotton trade along with population growth and infrastructure development made Mobile the place to live . . . and the place to pillage.

The halt to Mobile's burgeoning success arguably began in 1835 when a 12-year-old James Copeland stole a neighbor's pocketknife. His mother helped him cover up the crime and did so again when he was caught stealing pigs the same year. Because he'd been caught and faced incarceration, the pig theft posed a legitimate problem for the Copelands.

Incapable of letting her son suffer the consequences of his actions, Copeland's mother contacted her friend Gale Wages, leader of the notorious Wages Clan. Wages helped Copeland burn down the Jackson County Courthouse to destroy evidence of the case against Copeland, thus getting him out of paying for his crime.

Copeland moved to Mobile and with Wages's influence joined the Wages Clan, where he quickly rose to prominence. In 1939, Copeland was instrumental in robbing and destroying downtown Mobile. The clan docked boats at the port and employed six of their members as city guards to facilitate their thieving. The guards told the clan which stores had the best plunder.

---

Another Wages Clan plunder of $30,000 originally buried in Mobile's Hamilton Creek was relocated to Catahoula Swamp in 1846. Copeland never recovered it, so it allegedly remains to be found.

*A family walks out of Wet Willies, a popular downtown establishment that sits at the spot where Mobile's most infamous fires began.*

## WET WILLIES

**What:** The corner block where the Copeland fires allegedly began

**Where:** 200 Dauphin St.

**Cost:** Average $8

**Pro Tip:** Get your drink to go and take it out to Bienville Square to watch the squirrels—they're a bit nuts.

Just before midnight, when a new guard would take over, Copeland set fire to the robbed stores. Stiff winds carried the fire through the city. With the fire as a distraction, the gang continued robbing the city elsewhere, hauling wagonloads of stolen goods to the waiting boats throughout the night.

By morning, as the gang set sail for Dog River with $25,000 worth of stolen jewels, watches, silks, and more, a total of 600 buildings of French, British, and Spanish design, spanning blocks from Conception to Franklin, had been incinerated.

# RISE LIKE A PHOENIX

## What do fire stations and mystic societies have in common?

Mobile's modern-day firefighters have limited affiliation with Carnival. Barring riding at the end of each parade to signify its conclusion, there's little revelry in being a firefighter at Mardi Gras . . . but in the 1800s, fire stations were absolutely hopping.

April 9 is noted as being Fireman's Day, and back then it was more festive and better attended than Mardi Gras. Each company, with the exception of Creole Fire Company #1, who had their own celebration later, participated in the festivities. The Phoenix Steam Fire Company #6, formed in 1838, participated, as did nine others.

Each station aimed to outdo the others in terms of attire, decor, and overall festiveness. Brass bands were brought in from outside the city to lead each of the fire companies (there weren't enough bands for each company to have their own). Individual companies could spend as much as $1,000, and the total investment could reach as much as $10,000.

It sounds preposterous, but in the era of the volunteer firefighter, firefighting and reveling were of equal importance. Firehouses like Phoenix Steam Fire Company #6 had their horse-drawn steam fire engines downstairs and their ballrooms for revelry upstairs.

One firehouse, the Phoenix, was kept on to serve as the Phoenix Fire Museum. It was preserved along with an original

Mobile's history is littered with fires, but Mobile's fire companies were actually among the country's best. Lack of water and technology prohibited them from stopping the city's many destructive blazes.

*The April 9 Fireman's Day no longer exists, but firefighters make the most of their ride during Mardi Gras. Bucky Hicks waves from his fire truck on Fat Tuesday in 2020.*

## PHOENIX FIRE MUSEUM

**What:** Preserved historic Mobile fire museum (that's a little haunted)

**Where:** 203 S Claiborne St.

**Cost:** Free, but call 251-301-0270 to book a tour

**Pro Tip:** The museum is only open 9–5 Tuesdays through Fridays.

steam engine and other firehouse memorabilia. The second floor of the museum educates visitors about the life of a volunteer firefighter.

Employees on the second floor have heard footsteps and cabinets and doors opening. One employee confronted the spirit explaining procedural changes—like being closed on Mondays and having female employees. This talk allegedly calmed the spirit, but really . . . it's worth the tour to extinguish your burning curiosity, right?

# A MIGHTY OAK

**Can you really hear the winds whisper "I'm innocent; I'm innocent" at the tree where a man died?**

"I am innocent! But what can I do? When I am buried, an oak tree with a hundred roots will grow to prove my innocence."

Charles Boyington spoke these words in 1835 right before he was hanged for the murder of his friend Nathanial Frost.

The story goes that in 1933, 19-year-old Boyington moved to Mobile from Connecticut to work as a printer. Boyington lived in a boarding house with fellow printer Nathanial Frost.

## THE BOYINGTON OAK

**What:** Haunted, historic oak tree

**Where:** 107 S Bayou St.

**Cost:** Free

**Pro Tip:** Live oaks can live up to 500 years; the Boyington Oak has survived nearly two centuries of tropical weathering.

Like any other youth in an up-and-coming metro area, Boyington enjoyed a good time and was quite the gambler. Boyington had also taken a fancy to the lovely Rose de Fleur. While Rose seemingly returned Boyington's affections, her daddy didn't like that her paramour was poor and he made it difficult for them to liaise.

On May 11, 1835, Boyington asked Frost to help him carve a wooden heart as a gift for Rose. The two were seen together near Church Street Graveyard that afternoon. The same evening, Boyington asked his landlady to deliver a package to Rose. Boyington then boarded the *James Monroe* to sail for Montgomery. The following morning, Frost's body was found stabbed to death near the graveyard in an apparent robbery turned murder.

Boyington's absence and the fact that he'd been seen cavorting with Frost the night of his murder aroused immediate suspicion. It didn't help that Frost allegedly owed Boyington a

*Across from the Boyington Oak is the Big Zion AME Zion Church founded in 1842 by slaves. It's one of the oldest African American institutions in Mobile.*

gambling debt and that the carving knife the two were using was missing in action.

Boyington was arrested, tried, and hanged for murder. Before he died, he uttered his last words made famous by the oak tree that sprouted on the spot where he was laid to rest shortly after his death. The oak still stands tall and proud as a majestic testament to Boyington's declaration of innocence.

The Boyington Oak isn't the only significant tree in Mobile; the oaks at Bienville Square tell stories through art.

21

# SOUTHERN HISTORY MARKET

## What historic building did Mobile blow its budget on by 100 percent?

With 300-plus years since its foundation by the French, the Mobile we know today has a lot of history, and it's all encompassed in the History Museum of Mobile. Before that, it was in the Government Street Market; however, that space was so crowded and dirty that it was considered an embarrassment. Thus, the city, though in massive debt from the Creek War, fire damage, and the Panic of 1837, went ahead with plans to build the Italianate structure that stands today.

The Southern Market, which is reminiscent of today's Cathedral Square farmers markets that take place during the spring and fall, opened in 1858. Locals sold fish, fresh produce, fruit, and more in the space. Though the facility is gorgeous, it went over budget by 100 percent (oops). By 1875, the city of Mobile was so massively in debt (to the tune of $5 million) that it couldn't afford to make any kind of payments—not on principal nor interest.

Eventually, the building no longer hosted the market and instead housed entirely governmental buildings until Hurricane Frederic blew through in 1979. The hurricane came directly into Mobile Bay and destroyed a great deal of the city. It knocked out the Dauphin Island bridge entirely, and people had to take the ferry for a year to come and go.

### THE HISTORY MUSEUM OF MOBILE

**What:** Original site of the Southern Market and Old City Hall

**Where:** 111 S Royal St.

**Cost:** $5–$10, depending on age

**Pro Tip:** Take in the entire history of Mobile on a Gulf Coast Trolley Tour.

*The History Museum of Mobile, across from Mardi Gras Park, is adjacent to the Exploreum and Historic Fort Condé.*

In 2001, quite fittingly, the Southern Market and Old City Hall building came to house the History Museum of Mobile. Arguably, this is the place where Mobile all began—the fort located at the site where Mobile was established in 1711 is next door, and Mardi Gras Park, which celebrates Mobile's distinction as hosting the country's first Mardi Gras, is across the street.

Government offices were also housed in the Southern Market, which is why some also know it as Old City Hall. The second floor of the building was used to host dances.

# STEPPING BACK IN TIME

## What was life like for the wealthy in the 1800s?

Between fires (so many fires), the western migration of the 1900s, and the urban renewal of the 1960s, a *lot* of Mobile's most historic architecture was leveled, which is why the Oakleigh House Museum is such an invaluable relic (plus it's haunted, so there's that).

Built around 1833 by James Roper (there's also a Roper Street nearby), Oakleigh House was once a prominent and opulent Greek Revival–style home inhabited by the Roper family. Roper was a brickmaker from Virginia whose factory stood on the current site of today's historic Battle House Hotel. There were several other buildings on the sprawling property; however, when Roper's finances went south during the Panic of 1837, the property basically went, too.

Roper sold the other dwellings on his property as his finances tanked. Roper's brother-in-law purchased Oakleigh but let the Ropers continue living there.

Today's Oakleigh is a museum comprising a handful of structures: the Cox-Deasy Cottage is a former Creole cottage; the mansion itself has over 1,000 artifacts, including a wreath made of human hair (an old-fashioned form of memorial); and the Union Barracks, which were once thought to be cooks' quarters.

---

Roper's first wife and child died during the home's construction and may still be there. Ghost sightings, chill breezes, and objects moving on their own aren't uncommon at Oakleigh.

*Roper built the infamous staircase himself. Allegedly, the stairs and first-floor entry are the most haunted spots in the home.*

During the Civil War, to evade Oakleigh's destruction, the family hung the Union Jack to indicate they were neutral territory. Union soldiers built a four-room barrack on the property that local lore originally deemed as slave quarters; however, the age and architecture of the structure contradict this narrative . . . plus, when Roper lost his shirt, 18 of his 19 slaves were sold, and since much of his property was liquidated, it's likely any original dwellings for enslaved people were sold.

There's more to the story and to each of the period rooms in the mansion. It's a unique travel through time worth the wander.

## OAKLEIGH HOUSE MUSEUM

**What:** Mobile's oldest house museum

**Where:** 300 Oakleigh Pl.

**Cost:** $10 adults, $5 ages 5–16, free 5 and under and Historic Mobile Preservation Society members

**Pro Tip:** Tours, some of which are led by HMPS Mobile Belles, last an hour; the last tour starts at 3.

# IT WAS ALL YELLOW

## How did a Mobile doctor influence medical history?

Yellow fever swept into Mobile during the early 1700s with the arrival of the Pelican Girls and again at various points. It came with a vengeance in the 1830s. People assumed it was some kind of humidity or miasma causing the deadly illness. The worst year was 1839, when 600 are reported to have died, with thousands more made ill. The miserable ailment was characterized by fever, chills, black blood, and yellowed eyes.

A peculiar club called the Can't Get Away Club was formed. This unique society comprised Mobilians from all walks of life, who determined to stay and help those who were sick from the disease, regardless of who they were in society. They provided food and resources.

Though altruistic, the Can't Get Away Club essentially consisted of those who literally couldn't get away. Failure to flee the city at first whiff of the fever condemned one to stay put and ride it out; coincidentally, because the disease could not be spread person-to-person, staying on to help another wasn't as serious a risk as thought by CGA Club members.

Sadly, rises and falls in yellow fever epidemics wouldn't be quelled for at least two more decades. It wasn't until physician Josiah Nott, one of the founders of the Mobile Medical Society and the Medical College of Alabama, became extremely interested in yellow fever when four of his children died within

Josiah Nott's yellow fever breakthrough is sometimes overshadowed by his epigenetics studies, which suggested non-white races were "less human." Perpetuators of systemic racism clung to this "science" for some time.

*The museum boasts permanent and special collections, including a human remains collection.*

the span of a week during the 1853 epidemic. Nott suggested that mosquitoes perpetuated the fever. By the time William Crawford Georgas validated his theory and began making headway in eliminating yellow fever, Nott, along with 1,300 Mobilians, would be dead.

Today, the successes made regarding yellow fever and medical advents in general (locally, nationally, and internationally) are on interactive display at the Mobile Medical Museum.

# MOBILE MEDICAL MUSEUM

**What:** Historic medical museum with over 5,000 medical artifacts

**Where:** 1664 Springhill Ave.

**Cost:** $5 children 3+, $7 adults

**Pro Tip:** Staffing is limited, so call 251-415-1109 to make an appointment to visit.

# TAKE ME TO CHURCH

### Under what church were some in Church Street Cemetery originally buried?

The Church Street Cemetery next to the Ben May Mobile Public Library is one of Mobile's oldest and most famous. Many of its occupants ended their earthly journeys because of yellow fever. There are also some local celebrities—Joe Cain, the hero of Mobile's Mardi Gras, and Eugene Walter, Mobile's Renaissance man—who remain there.

Others have a more interesting post-life story. Cathedral Square is the grassy lawn in front of the Cathedral-Basilica of the Immaculate Conception. Prior to the cathedral's construction, there was a cemetery called Campo Santo on that spot. The cemetery was unkept, and the graves marked with simple wooden crosses were privy to livestock; thus, when the Church Street Cemetery opened in 1819, those at Campo Santo, which means "holy ground," were moved.

The cathedral was constructed over the course of several years. It was started in 1835, and Bishop Michael Portier consecrated it in 1850; however, it wouldn't be until the 1870s when the Doric order columns and portico were done and not until 1884 for the twin towers.

Lastly, the stained-glass windows, which were made in Munich, were installed starting in 1890. It may be divine intervention that these pieces of art weren't installed any sooner, as a famous munitions explosion on Mobile Bay

## CATHEDRAL OF THE IMMACULATE CONCEPTION

**What:** Historic Roman Catholic cathedral

**Where:** 2 S Claiborne St.

**Cost:** Free

**Pro Tip:** Pay homage to the spirits of the creative world at the Lupercalia Art Society after Mass; they're open 11–4 on Sundays.

*The Cathedral is an example of Greek Revival architecture. The iconic domes had to be repaired after sustaining damage during Hurricane Frederick in 1979.*

wreaked such havoc that the windows in the cathedral blew up, and, yes, it was the result of the munitions explosion.

There is no evidence of mysterious activity from Campo Santo in the cathedral, nor is there anything untoward about the crypt toward the front of the church where a number of bishops are laid to rest, presumably watching over the ever-faithful congregation.

It's claimed that the tunnels under the cathedral connect to those at the Lupercalia Art Society located just across Dauphin Street from the cathedral.

**29**

# HEALTH RESORT HILL

## Where can I get a little fresh air "for my health"?

In the late 1800s, following one of its worst yellow fever outbreaks, Mobile aimed to brand itself as a health resort. In an 1883 document for the Joint Committee of the Board of Trade and the Cotton Exchange, the merits of the Port City's tropical climate are touted as being a veritable panacea for malarial fever and other chronic ailments. The balmy air was claimed to carry iodine and bromine vapors that were "powerful tonics to the system."

Spring Hill, a relatively elevated area of Mobile, is cited specifically, and while calling Spring Hill a health resort is a bit of a stretch, a little time outdoors definitely does a body good, and there's no better place to get outdoors than Spring Hill.

Spring Hill College was founded by Mobile's first Catholic bishop, Michael Portier, and is the oldest college in Alabama. Uniquely, the college campus runs alongside the 18-hole par-72 Spring Hill Golf Course, which students actually have access to. In fact, you can get to the college from Dauphin Street by driving alongside the winding course.

If you're not into golf, then a walk among the oaks is always good for your health. One of Spring Hill College's most iconic features is called "The Avenue of the Oaks." The avenue, planted by Roger Stewart in 1850, is an almost half-mile drive

Behind Stewartfield is an exquisite Japanese magnolia that blooms each February. Japanese magnolias are Chinese trees that went through Japan and England before coming here.

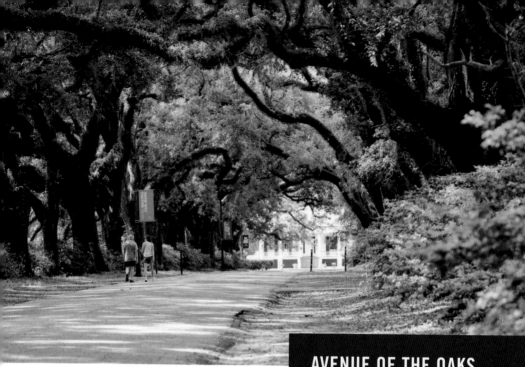

*The Avenue of the Oaks wasn't part of the original campus, but now it marks one of its borders and is used for graduation processions.*

that leads to Stewart's Greek Revival–style home of the same era, Stewartfield, which is now part of the campus.

It's a cherished destination for a romantic walk, a jog, a bike ride, or a quiet moment of reverence. While it may not cure your rheumatism as hopefuls in the 1800s suggest, it will certainly make you feel good.

## AVENUE OF THE OAKS

**What:** Landmark on the historic Spring Hill College campus

**Where:** Corner of Avenue of the Oaks and Magis Way

**Cost:** Free

**Pro Tip:** Walk across Old Shell Road for a latte and a scone from Carpe Diem, then walk the Avenue of the Oaks to the golf course, where you can sit on a bench and soak in the health benefits of the great outdoors.

# GANGSTER'S PARADISE, MAYBE

### Did the Copeland Gang have a secret hideout in Spring Hill?

The looting and burning of Mobile by the notoriously violent James Copeland and the Wages Clan is well documented. The Wages Clan burned 600 buildings of original Spanish, French, and British architecture in Mobile in October 1839.

Despite this, many historic homes still stand, and while the Yester House (a.k.a. the Dawson Perdue House and Carolina Hall) remains intact at 7 Yester Place, the allegedly haunted house isn't open to the public for tour.

Carolina Hall was built in 1832 by William A. Dawson. It's a Greek Revival–style home of Georgian antebellum influence, likely modeled after the one Dawson had in Charleston, South Carolina. It's also a historic home with one heck of a haunted history. First, there's the woman who was "accidentally" hanged in the home while it was being built. Many in the 1800s claimed to see a woman dancing around the front lawn like she was hanging from a rope.

There was also the man who was electrocuted on the home's iron fence in the backyard during a lightning storm (wrong place, wrong time?). Supposedly, during storms, some people see a man trying to escape the fence.

## CAROLINA HALL

**What:** Haunted Greek mansion in Spring Hill

**Where:** 7 Yester Pl.

**Cost:** Free

**Pro Tip:** Bring walking shoes and take a stroll or a jog around the area. You're just around the corner from the park, the Avenue of the Oaks at Spring Hill College, and Carpe Diem coffee.

*Yester House's style was adapted from the Tower of Winds in ancient Greece. The home is one of the stops on the Historic Spring Hill Driving Tour.*

Others have seen a woman looking out of the house through an upstairs window, which is impossible, as the home's upstairs windows are seven feet off the floor.

The final mysteries to Yester House are the secret, underground rooms discovered in the 1960s. Under the garden and fountain is a huge waterproof room and a 40-foot brick tunnel. Some suggest the Wages Clan used the tunnel as a hideout, but no links between Dawson or Copeland and the Wages Clan were indicated in Copeland's final accounts.

Mystery follows Dawson. A Mobile newspaper reported on December 5, 1899, that Josiah Small, an elderly African American man "raised by William A. Dawson," was found murdered.

# LIVING HISTORY IN AFRICATOWN

## Where's the only settlement started and run by Africans in the US?

In the cover of darkness on July 9, 1860, just off 12 Mile Island on the Mobile River, the schooner *Clotilda*, the last-known American slave ship, was set ablaze to mask evidence of a felony.

The crime was a carefully orchestrated plot by wealthy landowner Timothy Meaher, a vaunter who believed the federal government's enforcement of the Slave Trade Act of 1807, which prohibited new slave importations, would bankrupt the South. Per lore, Meaher placed a bet that he could import newly enslaved people right under the government's watchful eye without being caught.

Despite the penalty for such sedition being death, Meaher contracted Captain William Foster for the job, and in March of 1860, the *Clotilda* departed Mobile en route to West Africa's Kingdom of Dahomey.

Foster returned with just over 100 captives. He and Meaher disguised the *Clotilda* as a barge and towed it, undetected, to 12 Mile Island by moonlight. Once the ship had been emptied, Foster burned it, destroying evidence of its use for slave trading.

Investors in the voyage were compensated with captives; Meaher kept 30 individuals for himself, including Cudjoe Lewis, who, in 1931, recounted his memoirs to Zora Neale Hurston;

In 2019, the long-sought-after remains of the *Clotilda* were unearthed by journalist Ben Raines, giving proof of the ship's existence and of the illicit journey, something that had been previously denied by many.

*Though Africatown attracted other Africans, some in the community were isolated from and shamed because of their unique heritage; however, preserving and reviving the community is increasingly important.*

Lewis's story offers a rare glimpse into the brutal experience of being captured and of the harrowing transatlantic voyage.

The *Clotilda* slaves were emancipated following the Civil War but without funds to return home—their most ardent desire. Instead, they purchased Magazine Point at Plateau, where they'd initially landed the night the *Clotilda* illicitly arrived in Mobile.

Here, Lewis and others established Africatown, the first independently run community of Africans in the US. Until the 1950s, the community operated based on Takpa tribal customs. Of the original settlement, the Union Baptist Church, Plateau Cemetery, and the Africatown Community remain at the original site.

## DORA FRANKLIN FINLEY AFRICAN-AMERICAN HERITAGE TRAIL

**What:** Guided tour of iconic African American landmarks

**Where:** 111 S Royal St.

**Book:** 251-725-2236 for guided; www.mobilehd.org/aaht for self-guided

**Cost:** $40 adults, $30 students, $20 seniors and children 17 and under; self-guided FREE

**Pro Tip:** Pay your respects to Cudjoe Lewis, whose grave is marked by an obelisk at the Plateau Africatown Historic Cemetery.

# HOODOO YOU DO?

## Where can I find the Queen of Hoodoo?

I know what you're thinking . . . you find the Queen of Hoodoo in New Orleans . . . or somewhere in a parish swamp not far from there. Actually, the Queen of Hoodoo, globally known as Her Imperial Grace Queen Cotaliya Benson Milner-Meadows de la Pound, resides and practices in Mobile.

The queen who goes by Queen Co (thanks for that) practices hoodoo magic that's been prominent in her family for over 400 years. Queen Co explains that most African Americans in the US descend from people who came through the Port of Mobile, which gives this area a history and an energy and is why her practice exists here.

The magic Queen Co practices in her apothecary and divination space, known as Conjure South, is the tradition brought by Africans to the Americas starting in the 1600s. Because the customs of Africans were scorned, they were disguised and adapted into the Africans' new lives as what's today known as hoodoo.

> **CONJURE SOUTH**
>
> **What:** The Hoodoo Queen's shop
>
> **Where:** 10 S Conception St.
>
> **Cost:** Average $15 for crystals, incense, and powders; average $35–$60 for other
>
> **Pro Tip:** Schedule card readings and other divination practices online in advance; scheduling is available on the conjuresouth.com website.

Hoodoo is distinct from religion; it's called a "conjure," which is a term referring to spiritual casting to achieve a means, often positive. People who aren't practitioners or who have little exposure may find this confusing, but that's okay. Queen Co uses social media to educate and to reach a wider audience.

After all, one doesn't have to practice hoodoo to benefit from a visit to Conjure South, as there are many herbs, oil, candles, roots, and other resources that can help with

*Hoodoo Queen Co films content for social media near Conjure South, her apothecary and divination space designed to help people connect spiritually and heal.*

whatever ailments you have. Some people—even religious ones, including leaders—seek the divinity of hoodoo queens when they feel at a loss.

Speaking of loss, Queen Co does assist with those who have lost, helping people find healing and recognizing how loved ones communicate when they're beyond this life. Here, many religious people may find they understand a little hoodoo after all.

Eating black-eyed peas on New Year's Day is a form of hoodoo. Black-eyed peas, which are indigenous to Africa, were the Africans' traditions.

# CYCLING THROUGH HISTORY

## How can I take a ride on the Underground Railroad?

The Underground Railroad was the secret passage used by African Americans to escape slavery. Being largely wet and low elevation, the Gulf Coast isn't home to many tunnels, but Mobile was a starting point on the legendary Underground Railroad (UGRR) to freedom.

The UGRR Adventure Cycling route spans 1,997.1 miles and takes you from Mobile to Ontario, Canada, in a series of five historic stopping points along the way. A map on the Adventure Cycling app leads to key stops and indicates other important UGRR stops.

In the early 1900s, though, while there was a map, the risk of being caught was ever-present, and the consequences could be life-ending. Thus, a clever folk song called "Follow the Drinking Gourd" was shared to guide enslaved people to freedom.

While a drinking gourd refers to a hollowed gourd that enslaved African Americans used to dip water, in the song, the gourd is actually the celestial Big Dipper. The "ole man" in the song is Peg Leg Joe, one of the Underground Railroad operators, who encoded the map and created the song.

The second verse details the journey's start from Mobile to northern Alabama. "The riva's bank am a very good road," refers

One stop in Spanish Fort is at Meaher State Park. The park was donated to Alabama by the Meahers, descendants of Timothy Meaher, who commissioned the *Clotilda*.

*The first stop is at one of the slave markets, which stood on the northwest corner of Royal and St. Louis Streets. A sign explains that this is the site where Clotilda slaves arrived in August 1859.*

## SLAVE MARKETS

**What:** First stop on the UGRR cycling experience

**Where:** Northwest corner of Royal and St. Louis Streets

**Cost:** $9.99 for each part of the map via app

**Pro Tip:** Take a detour to Michael Donald Rd. off Old Shell Rd. The 1981 lynching of Donald was the last known lynching by KKK members in the US.

to the Tombigbee River, which empties into Mobile Bay.

"The dead trees show the way, Lef' foot, peg foot goin' on," are lines about how Peg Leg Joe marked trees and other landmarks with charcoal or mud. He used the outline of a human left foot and a round spot in place of a right foot to indicate the route.

The route starts at one of the marked sites of the former slave markets in Mobile. It shows other sites (like the Zion Church next to the Boyington Oak on Bayou Street) up the river to Africatown and beyond.

# THE ENDANGERED FORT

### Can I see one of America's best-preserved Civil War forts?

When we talk about endangered things, we're usually talking about animal species, but just like they say Venice is sinking, erosion around Dauphin Island is endangering Fort Gaines. Thankfully, though, the fort, which is one of the nation's best-preserved Civil War forts, is still intact (for now) and open daily for touring.

Fort Gaines was constructed in 1821 because the US thought it would be smart to have robust defenses flanking the bay (Gaines's sister fort, Fort Morgan, is just across the bay). In fact, the US spent several million on the forts, knowing that if they failed to keep enemies out they could be powerful assets for those enemies. Obviously, no one anticipated that in a few short decades the fort would be used how the US both hoped and feared.

In 1861, just ahead of plans to secede from the Union, the state of Alabama sent infantry to occupy Fort Gaines. The batteries at Dauphin Island and Fort Morgan held strong until August 1864, when David Farragut led the Union to victory in the Battle of Mobile Bay. Over a thousand Union soldiers landed on Dauphin Island while Union fire lambasted the fort from the water. On August 8, the Confederacy surrendered Fort Gaines.

## HISTORIC FORT GAINES

**What:** One of the nation's best-preserved battle forts

**Where:** 51 Bienville Blvd., Dauphin Island

**Cost:** $6 for 13 and over; $4 for children 5–12

**Pro Tip:** Check the Fort Gaines Historic Site Facebook page for upcoming events before you visit.

*Many features at Fort Gaines, like the cannon, are authentic relics used during the battle hundreds of years ago.*

Today, the fort is well preserved. A kitchen and blacksmith shop still stand with blacksmith demonstrations happening regularly. There are also reenactments throughout the year; the most popular is the annual Thunder on the Bay, which takes place in April and spectacularly recreates Fort Gaines's role in the Battle of Mobile Bay. Full speed ahead!

Some say the fort is haunted; pockets of cold air in the arched brick tunnels and the distant giggles of children have been reported by tourists.

# DAMN THE TORPEDOES!

## Why is there an underwater graveyard in Mobile Bay?

Though it's been nearly 200 years since, the Civil War and area battles still loom large in Mobile. To be fair, there's a *lot* to unpack. One of the most notorious skirmishes was the Battle of Mobile Bay, which was a decisive battle that dealt a fatal blow to the Confederacy and was the first step in securing a Union victory for the whole enchilada.

In the battle, Union Admiral David Farragut (enlisted since age nine, which offers a stark contrast to today's Minecraft generation) approached Mobile Bay in August 1864 with a fleet of 18 ships. The ships faced four Confederate ships, which included the most powerful ironclad at sea, the CSS *Tennessee*, along with the batteries flanking Mobile Bay at Fort Gaines and Fort Morgan. It was (almost) literally David versus Goliath.

On August 5, Farragut *literally* damned the torpedoes assaulting his fleet and blasted into the bay, taking out the vital batteries that made the bay area such a formidable Confederate stronghold.

The *Tecumseh*, however, was struck and sunk; 93 souls went down with the ship, which became lost in Mobile Bay . . . or so it was thought. Sonny Wintzell, founder of the eponymous oyster bar, spent $15,000 to find the vessel. In 1967, the Smithsonian wanted to dig it up, but Sonny felt sure they wouldn't find it. By accident, they did.

---

Hatchett Chandler's dying wish to be buried at Fort Morgan was ruled against. His friends buried him 90 feet from the battery wall in an illicit shotgun funeral anyway.

*The Mobile Bay Ferry takes passengers across the waters where the Battle of Mobile Bay played out in 1864.*

Thus, a different kind of battle ensued—local Hatchett Chandler took up the fight, insisting *Tecumseh* belonged at Fort Morgan, but he died days after the case was dismissed.

In the end, parts of the ship were salvaged and directed to various museums for preservation. The rest remain protected by ordinance of the US Navy in a marked underwater graveyard in the bottom of Mobile Bay.

## MOBILE BAY FERRY

**What:** Aquatic passage to Fort Morgan from Dauphin Island

**Where:** 112 Bienville Blvd., Dauphin Island

**Cost:** $6 for pedestrians and bicycles; $7 for motorcycles; $15–20 for vehicles

**Pro Tip:** Call 251-861-3000 to make sure the ferry is running before you go; they will not operate on stormy or windy days.

# MOBILE'S BIGGEST BOOM-BOOM

## What really happened in the explosion heard around the US?

The day was May 25, 1965, and the Civil War had been won; Mobile had surrendered to avoid destruction (a little ironic when you consider what happened next). Because Mobile was a port city and thus a great avenue for shipping munitions to the army inland, the Union garrison was storing confiscated Confederate ammunition at a warehouse off Commerce and Lipscomb Streets, near Beauregard.

It's said that Confederates were under orders to move some of the munitions, which consisted of 200 tons of explosives, gunpowder, and ammunition, but, allegedly, former slaves who had limited experience handling such materials were given the onerous task. Then, something ignited. A plume of black smoke billowed over the warehouse depot. The ground shook, and suddenly, BOOM!

The sky burst open with flames shooting up from the ground and timber, cotton, people, and horses scattered throughout downtown Mobile. An entire eight square blocks of the city were leveled; two steamers sank. The cost of the munitions was estimated to be $8 million. Initial reports were that 500 were killed, but that was updated to 300. Newspapers around the

---

### SECRET HISTORY TOURS

**What:** Walking tours that reveal the secret history of Mobile

**Where:** www.secrethistorytours.com

**Cost:** Average $25

**Pro Tip:** Bring extra cash; tours don't include cocktails, but you can buy them at stops as part of the experience.

*The historic Mobile GM&O Building stands at the road where the depot exploded. Guests of Todd Duren's Secret History Tours visit sites such as this and learn about the past.*

country reported the tragedy with a ghastly description of body parts raining down over the devastated city.

A sizable crater was left in the wake of the devastation and remained for some time as a memorial to those who died in the tragedy.

---

The blast was so magnificent that it blew the windows out of the Cathedral of the Immaculate Conception, which is nine diagonal square blocks from where the depot stood.

# OH, DEER!

## Why is there a deer in Washington Square Park?

Mobile's Washington Square Park is the darling of the Oakleigh District. Surrounded by live oak trees and Victorian-style cottages, the square, which was named by its benefactor Archibald Gordon in 1850 (two decades before the better-known one in New York City was thusly named), is a favorite place for strolling and enjoying the outdoors.

The park's central feature is a beautiful fenced-in fountain. As with Bienville Square, the surrounding sidewalk converges to the center of the grassy oak-lined square.

One of the square's features does stand out. A cast iron deer statue is on the Palmetto Street side of the square, and while many photograph the deer and climb on it, few know its history.

The deer was originally at a home on Springhill Avenue. The deer had a sister deer and the two stood together on the lawn of George A. Tuthill Sr. along with statues of two African American boys who were positioned as if tending to the deer. The four statues were considered some of the finest cast iron works in all of Mobile, and they were Tuthill's greatest pride.

Unfortunately for Tuthill, after the last major skirmishes of the Civil War, Union troops infiltrated Mobile. Upon coming to the Tuthill home, a Union officer stopped the progress and announced that the statues of the enslaved boys were "an affront to our cause." He decided they should free them from

---

**WASHINGTON SQUARE PARK**

**What:** Historic park in the Oakleigh District

**Where:** 251 Chatham St.

**Cost:** Free

**Pro Tip:** Washington Square Park is two blocks from Callaghan's Irish Social Club, so if you get hungry, head toward Marine and Charleston Streets for a nibble.

*Few know the story of the Washington Square Park deer. Many sit on her for a photo, and during Mardi Gras she is decorated so as not to feel left out.*

their bondage, so the Union soldiers moved the statues from the yard and hauled them down to the Mobile River, where they were cast into the abyss.

Tuthill was in a dither and spent thousands of dollars in an effort to recover his precious artwork. He was only able to recover one of the statues, a single deer, now serving as the lone sentinel of Washington Square Park.

Archibald Gordon never had children. When he died, he left $5,000 to his former slave. Gordon is buried aboveground in the Church Street Graveyard.

# THE UNRECONSTRUCTED REBEL

## Who was the first woman writer to break $100,000 in sales?

In the early 1800s, it was relatively unheard of for women to be writers, let alone successful ones, and yet romantic moralist Augusta Evans accomplished both (without using a pen name, no less). Despite being professionally progressive, Evans held deep contempt for the North. It was these views that earned her the Unreconstructed Rebel nickname.

While she wasn't defensive of the South per se, nor of slavery, she did deride the North's capitalistic priority and their cold and indifferent nature. She identified the South as having heart and beauty and ultimately favored secession. Her politics were prominent in her writings, and they soon sold very well, allowing her to buy her family a home on Springhill Avenue called Georgia Cottage.

Because of her sympathies, the writer volunteered as a nurse for Civil War soldiers. While doing so, she published a book that may have been one of the earliest banned books. Published in 1862, the work called *Macaria: Altars of Sacrifice*, while arguably neither overtly anti-Union nor anti-North, was decidedly pro-South. The book, which was popular in both the North and the South, was burned by General George Henry Thomas.

The book was later bootlegged, but when Evans's publisher found out, he confronted the bootlegger and had all of the royalties put into a trust that Evans would receive after the war.

---

## MAGNOLIA CEMETERY

**What:** Historic Mobile cemetery

**Where:** 1202 Virginia St.

**Cost:** Free

**Pro Tip:** Augusta Evans Wilson is located at Range K-Lot 33.

*The Magnolia Street Cemetery is Mobile's third-oldest cemetery and is where many other well-known people like Josiah Nott, the Bellingraths, and Apache Indian Chappo Geronimo are buried.*

It was a sizable amount; though, it was her 1866 romance, *St. Elmo*, that made her truly wealthy when over 40 million copies sold in four months.

While Evans kept writing, she also devoted efforts to helping Confederate soldiers rest in peace at home. A section of the Magnolia Cemetery on Virginia Street was designated for that cause. Upon her death, Evans's substantial fortune was donated to help establish the Mobile Infirmary and St. Francis Methodist Church.

Evans's 960 Government St. home was torn down in 1911 to make way for an Edwardian-style luxury apartment complex called the Antoinette.

# JOE CAIN AND THE PEOPLE'S WALKING PARADE

## Where can you see the entire culture and history of Mobile in a single day?

One of the biggest differences between Mobile's Mardi Gras and New Orleans's is Joe Cain Day. Cain is credited with reviving the Mardi Gras tradition in Mobile after the Civil War. He was a volunteer firefighter at Washington No. 8 who was invited to parade with a New Orleans fire department in our dear sister city in 1867.

By his own account, Cain had such a pleasant time in New Orleans that "I determined on my return home, that Mobile should have its own Mobile Mardi Gras celebration."

Thus, in 1868, Joseph Stillwell Cain took to the streets with his Lost Cause Minstrels. Local lore has it that Cain dressed up as Chickasaw Indian Chief Slacabamorinico and paraded in a charcoal wagon to a cacophony of music just ahead of the Order of the Myths parade.

While technically Joe Cain only resuscitated Mardi Gras by just a few hours, he's credited with the whole shebang. Joe Cain Day takes place the Sunday before Fat Tuesday and is characterized by rebellion and revelry (Joe Cain would've wanted it that way).

---

**THE JOE CAIN SUNDAY PEOPLE'S PARADE**

**What:** Free Mardi Gras parade for the people

**Where:** Parade route A

**Cost:** Your dignity

**Pro Tip:** Never bend over to pick up a throw unless you want to get clonked upside the head with a MoonPie (or a pack of Conecuh sausage).

*The Nevergreens wear only purple and gold and give playful citations to parade-goers donning green (Mobile's official Mardi Gras colors are purple and gold . . . never green).*

It's free to participate in the People's Parade and, traditionally, individual floats and wagons follow Chief Slacabamorinico's procession through downtown Mobile. In the past decade, the walking parade has gained traction with festive groups boasting cultural or historical ties to Mobile. Picture pirates, Pelican Girls, a pot of gumbo, some Nevergreens, a band of secret misters, and monstrous women and you've got the idea.

This rambunctious parade is a platform for openly defying social hierarchies and exclusionary practices, and we are here for it.

Much of the Mobile Mardi Gras story is legend and lore, but luckily people here don't want proof . . . they just want to party. So, do as we do and say as we say and *laissez les bon temps rouler*!

Allegedly, America's first Carnival was held by Mobile's Société de Boeuf Gras in 1702. They rolled paper mâché bull heads around like matadors; we're not sure why. Alcohol was involved.

# MAKING WIDOWS MERRY

## Did Joe Cain really have a bunch of widows and mistresses?

If you've spent enough time around Mobile, then you've undoubtedly heard of Joe Cain Day and Cain's "merry widows." If you've attended a Joe Cain parade, then you'll have seen the procession of black-clad mystery women, all members of a secret society called Cain's Merry Widows, parade behind Joe Cain.

The irony behind Cain's Merry Widows is that the real Joseph Cain had only one wife, Elizabeth; however, it's not much of a parading society if there's only one widow, so now the women (we assume they're all women) don all black and disguise their true identities, adopting monikers like "Savannah" and "Magnolia" (delightfully syrupy Southern names) and grieve their way through the streets of Mobile in loving honor of their dearly departed Joe Cain.

It's deliciously farcical theater that begins long before the parades begin on the Sunday ahead of Mardi Gras. At 8 a.m., the widows greet runners who (against their better judgment) convene at the corner of Broad and Canal for the Joe Cain Classic 5K.

Of course, the widows' official duties start at Joe Cain's grave at Church Street Cemetery, where they argue over who Cain loved the most, then they proceed to Joe Cain's childhood

---

In the 1830s, real Mobilians widowed by disease were provided housing along Elmira Street courtesy of the Female Benevolent Society. Later, Civil War widows were housed at Murray Hall.

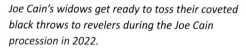

*Joe Cain's widows get ready to toss their coveted black throws to revelers during the Joe Cain procession in 2022.*

home to join the runners for a street party. They toast to Joe Cain with champagne and make merry with crowds and one another before the parade, where they're likely to clash with the Mistresses of Joe Cain.

In 2003, a group of mystery women clad in red joined the fun; the mistresses and the widows mock catfight, claiming that Joe loved *them* the best. It's all jest and all in good fun and—barring the champagne part— not much like real widowhood, thankfully, which isn't merry at all. Thank goodness for tomfoolery.

## THE MERRY WIDOW

**What:** Bar and music hall named for Cain's Merry Widows

**Where:** 51 S Conception St.

**Cost:** Average $5

**Pro Tip:** The bar manager's recipes are inspired by her time in South Korea, and many drinks, like the Crybaby Bridge, nod to local lore.

# EXPLORING NEW TRADITIONS

### What's so special about Mobile's first integrated Mardi Gras society?

There's an inevitable moment of cringe when children who grew up screaming "Throw me something, mister!" at Mardi Gras parades realize that most of the mystic societies are still segregated.

It's not immediately obvious if you're attending Mardi Gras for some beads and MoonPies, but Mobile has two Mardi Gras organizations: the Mobile Area Mardi Gras Association (MAMGA) for African Americans and the Mobile Carnival Association (MCA). Both associations have kings and queens, and it wasn't until the first decade of the 21st century that the African American king and queen attended the MCA royal ball.

This segregation has been called the last bastion of Jim Crow, which locals take issue with. Many of both races advocate for sticking with doing things the way they've always been done, claiming to like the distinction of the way each organization celebrates. While there's a lot to be said for tradition, it's what underpins the tradition that raises flags for others.

Thus, in 2004, an organization broke ranks with tradition and formed Mobile's first integrated Mardi Gras society. The Condé Explorers was formed because—per the 2008 *Order of Myths* documentary featured on Amazon Prime—a parade-

Mobile's first gay society, Order of Osiris, held its first dance in 1980. Osiris is now considered the best ball to attend, because of their wildly entertaining tableau.

*Dancers performs in the Knights of Revelry procession on Fat Tuesday in 2022.*

goer was disheartened when his son wasn't favored with throws during a parade. He decided something had to be done, so he founded Mobile's first integrated society. The group now has a diverse population of males and females of all races.

The takeaway from the establishment of the Condé Explorers is that the tradition of Mardi Gras can still exist but without the antiquated prejudices retained from a bygone era. While Mobile's Mardi Gras tradition is the oldest, New Orleans was first to prohibit any kind of biases in organizations; hopefully, Mobile will follow suit sooner than later.

## MOBILE CARNIVAL MUSEUM

**What:** Mardi Gras history museum located in historic Bernstein-Bush mansion

**Where:** 355 Government St.

**Cost:** $3 student groups and children under 12; $6 military; $8 adults

**Pro Tip:** Plan ahead. The museum is only open 9–4 on Mondays, Wednesdays, Fridays, and Saturdays.

# OH BABY CAKES (THE NEXT ONE'S ON YOU)

## Where can I find the best king cake in Mobile?

First, I'm not answering that question because it's a trick. King cake is subjective. Also, there's possibly a King Cake Mafia. (If you've learned nothing else about Mobile, you know that Mobilians love secret societies, so a King Cake Mafia is bound to happen if it hasn't already. Presumably, the threats will be issued in the form of tiny plastic baby Jesuses).

All jesting aside, there really are babies in the king cakes. If you are at a gathering and you get the baby, provided you don't choke to death, you're obligated to bring the cake to next year's gathering, and there is a *lot* of pressure because you do *not* want to show up with a *bad* king cake. You may as well have just choked on the baby when you had a chance.

> ### THE LIGHTHOUSE BAKERY
>
> **What:** Dauphin Island bakery and diner
>
> **Where:** 919 Chaumont Ave., Dauphin Island
>
> **Cost:** A week of calories; $30+ for a full cake, depending on size
>
> **Pro Tip:** The king cakes are larger than your average king cake, so order wisely. Visit the bakery anytime. Sunday mornings, they make crabmeat omelets.

(Has anyone ever tried to swallow the baby? Asking for myself.)

Because it *is* so hard to determine which baby is indeed the best, Mobile has orchestrated a delicious competition that takes place at the forefront of each Mardi Gras called the King Cake-Off. Locals vote on the best entry for ultimate bragging rights.

Buy *why* do we do king cake for Mardi Gras? It all has to do with the 12 days of Christmas.

The 12 days of Christmas transpire in the 12 days after December 25. The 12th day, January 6, is marked with the

*The amaretto cream cheese–filled king cake from Lighthouse Bakery is large enough to feed a crowd (and still have some left over!). All of the pastries at Lighthouse Bakery are festive during Mardi Gras. Photo courtesy of Greg Vrachalus*

Feast of the Epiphany. It's called King's Day, for that's when the three wise men arrived to bestow gifts on the newborn baby Jesus. King's Day marks the official beginning of Carnival season, and sympathetic revelers feast on king cake from then until midnight on Mardi Gras Day.

Then Lent begins, and we start using those gym memberships we gave ourselves for Christmas.

Built in the 1920s as a grand lodge to the Scottish Rite Bodies, the Temple, which is the site of the King Cake-Off, is architecturally modeled after the Egyptian pyramids.

# MOONPIE OVER MOBILE

## Where can I try a MoonPie?

If you spend New Year's Eve in Mobile, then you know we count down to each New Year to the drop of a MoonPie. Considering MoonPies are from Chattanooga, this tradition doesn't make much sense . . . a crawfish would make more sense, right?

MoonPies are marshmallow-filled cookies covered in chocolate. The flavors have grown from the original cream and chocolate to include mint chocolate, banana, orange vanilla, and more. MoonPies are now an incredibly popular throw at Mardi Gras—hundreds of thousands are flung into eager crowds each year.

Since Mobile hosted the first Mardi Gras parade in the 1700s (back when it was called *Bouef Gras* and celebrations involved pushing a cart carrying a papier-mâché cow head down the road), it logically follows that the New Year's celebration tie into our city's most cherished claim to fame.

But still . . . why MoonPies and not beads or a bust of Joe Cain or Cracker Jack boxes? Actually, Cracker Jack was the reason MoonPies were brought in as throws. In the '40s and '50s, members of one of the ladies' organizations expressed concerns over the injurious hard corners of otherwise delicious boxes of Cracker Jack.

During a convention in Chattanooga, the women came upon the sweet treat we all know and love as MoonPies. MoonPies are soft and as satisfying to eat as Cracker Jack, but they don't

---

The MoonPie over Mobile celebration started in 2008 and is a night of celebration with fireworks, live music, and more. Trombone Shorty showed up to help Mobile ring in 2022!

*A giant MoonPie hangs over downtown Mobile year-round just as Toomey's Mardi Gras, where many riders get their throws, is open all year.*

hurt people who might miss a well-intended throw. Plus, the women liked that MoonPies had a little heft to them, which meant that they could lob them through the crowds during a parade.

Another thing is that MoonPies are distinct from New Orleans. Our Carnivals have much in common, but MoonPies . . . that's all Mobile, and that's why every December 31, Mobilians gather downtown to celebrate the promise of a new year with the MoonPie over Mobile.

## TOOMEY'S MARDI GRAS

**What:** The ultimate year-round Mardi Gras store in Mobile

**Where:** RSA 755 McRae Ave.

**Cost:** $5 for a small box of MoonPies

**Pro Tip:** For the ultimate Southern indulgence, eat your MoonPie with a scoop of Cammie's Old Dutch ice cream.

# AND THE BEAT GOES ON

## What's the oldest, continuous band in America?

While most people hear Creoles and think Louisiana, Mobile actually has a significant and long-established population of Creoles. The Catholic churches maintained baptismal, death, and marriage records, which track Creole lineage in Mobile almost from the time of the city's establishment by the French.

The term Creole refers specifically to anyone not Native American. A shortage of white women and support for interracial relationships by the dominant European culture of the day and the Catholic Church led to a large Creole population in Mobile.

Because Creoles observed many of the same rights as white citizens, proof of one's Creole heritage—especially for Creoles of color—was important. Leading up to the 1850s, the Creole population grew significantly, but an influx of Puritans, whose beliefs contradicted existing social norms, stymied Creole population growth and threatened local Creoles' freedom.

To keep themselves distinguished and safer against prejudices and injustices projected on African Americans, Creoles formed organizations, including the Creole Social Club and the Creole Fire Company. The Creole Fire Company #1 was formed in 1819. In 1869, the company moved into the two-story brick structure that still stands downtown (the historic structure is now a private residence).

The venue was more than a firehouse; it was also used by the Creole Fire Company organization for entertainment and

Many Creole families still reside at Mon Louis Island off Fowl River. Creole culture and traditions are preserved at this 18th-century French settlement.

*The Excelsior Band and the Bloom House Band entertain during the 2022 Knights of Revelry parade on Royal Street in Mobile.*

## CREOLE FIRE STATION #1

**What:** Original location where the Excelsior Band was formed in 1883

**Where:** 13 N Dearborn St.

**Cost:** Free

**Pro Tip:** The Excelsior Band is the oldest continuous band in the US.

business. Members hosted events and weddings and played music there.

In 1883, in celebration of the birth of his son, musician John A. Pope and his band played all night long. It was that night that the Excelsior Band was formed. The Excelsior Band is a 10-piece brass band still going strong. You can see them in nearly all the Mardi Gras parades. The exclusive band also performs for weddings, receptions, events, and more around Mobile and the rest of Alabama.

# ALL THAT JAZZ

## Where's a hot place to listen to cool music?

There are a lot of great bands and musical artists in Mobile, and you can catch them most any night of the week around town, but way back in the day, Mobile used to have some serious brass bands. Today, you can listen to the Excelsior Band and the Olympia Band, which has made a comeback. Still, for years, Mobile was bereft of a solid jazz club.

Of course, Mobile is known for a lot of things, but jazz isn't one of them, even though "the Martin Luther King of music" was born in Mobile. James Europe was born in 1881. He was an innovative and bold musician making waves for both African Americans and musically.

Europe's music career took off when he was in New York. There, he formed the Clef Club, which was the first group of African American artists to play proto jazz at Carnegie Hall; they were also the first to be recorded, in 1913. Europe formed a band, the Harlem Hellfighters, during his service in World War I and toured afterward. His ragtime jazz music was exceptional because it was unlike anything else being done, and it hasn't been replicated since, according to those who know.

Europe's art was about fusion and culture, which another modern-day Mobilian is seemingly embracing at Kazoola Eatery and Entertainment. Kazoola is Mobile's only jazz bar, but what's even more intriguing is the local history.

## KAZOOLA

**What:** Late-night jazz bar named for *Clotilda* survivor Cudjoe Lewis

**Where:** 558 Dauphin St.

**Cost:** Average menu price $10

**Pro Tip:** Nod to the city that launched Europe's illustrious musical career with a NY sour, a (jazz) riff on a whiskey sour. (Everybody scat now.)

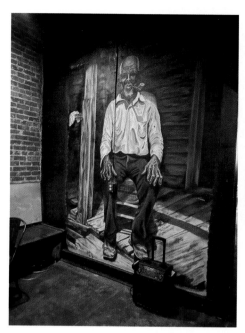

*Guests enjoy cold drinks and dance the night away at Kazoola. Photo courtesy of Kazoola*

Kazoola is owned by Marc Jackson. Jackson grew up in Africatown, and though he started a successful career in finance, his heart yearned for jazz. The name of the venue honors his heritage; Kazoola is the pronunciation of Cudjoe Lewis's given African name.

The way Jackson is bringing his story, culture, and passion together . . . it's exactly what jazz is all about. It's a tune only he can carry, and it sounds good.

Kazoola pays homage to B.B. King's Blues Club. The hot spot, which is open late, is a fusion of jazz, blues, and Motown.

# PROHIBITED PORT CITY IMPORTS

## Were Mobilians really a bunch of bootleggers?

The Colonial Era in Mobile was characterized by hard work and even harder relaxation (booze, we mean booze) . . . but the great state of Alabama didn't think that this was such a great idea and imposed draconian "bone dry" laws in 1915 (five years before the 18th Amendment was ratified to prohibit the national manufacture, distribution, and sale of alcohol).

Mobilians took one look at the newly imposed legislation and said, "It's a no for me." Despite the largely unilateral concurrence that Prohibition wasn't happening here, the imposition of laws and punishments and stuff meant clandestine boozing became de rigueur.

Men and women alike aided and abetted the illicit cause, which largely entailed bringing in suds from Cuba and England via the Port of Mobile. Women helped by driving in such a way that blocked law officers from catching bootleggers (fiddle-dee-dee!) and using feminine wiles to throw Johnny Law off the proverbial trail.

Meanwhile, the gents went here, there, and yonder in order to bring a bottle (or tens of thousands of bottles) home for national distribution. Mobile's boozy network laced as far north as Chicago.

While many prominent Mobilians pop up in this sordid tale, one directly ties to a local space that hosts a top-tier brunch.

### RUBY SLIPPER CAFÉ

**What:** Restaurant owned by bootlegger in the Mobile Bank Building

**Where:** 100 N Royal St.

**Cost:** Varies

**Pro Tip:** Mobile still prohibits the sale of alcohol on a Sunday before noon.

*The Ruby Slipper Café, a New Orleans–born restaurant where bootlegging was also rampant, is best-known for brunches, Bloody Marys, and mimosas.*

The then Mobile Bank, located off the Port of Mobile, was presided over by Alfred L. Staples. In 1919, just before federal Prohibition mandates, Staples, along with Frank Boykin, a prominent politico and bootlegger, was named director of the Mobile Shipbuilding Company.

Even if the bank building wasn't used for marauding liquor, the connection between the locale and Staples stands, which makes today's Ruby Slipper Café a historic space to slide into for cochin benedict and a cocktail (before noon on a Sunday if you're into flouting antiquated laws).

The Prohibition Era also saw another import through the Port of Mobile—red fire ants. They were brought in from ships from South America. Respectfully, the rum was better.

# WALK SOFTLY, SPEAKEASY

## Are there really tunnels hidden under Mobile?

Despite legalese, Mobile was a hub for an international bootlegging ring that reached to Chicago. The Port City was especially well connected with the Caribbean, and there was a well-orchestrated smuggling network there in which illicit liquors from Cuba and the Bahamas would be brought in, stored in garages, and then distributed. Imported liquors would either be disguised in turpentine barrels and shipped north or distributed around the city for local distribution. The business run by this ring was so prolific that the demand outstripped the supply.

When this organization was caught, 70 men of varying positions of high influence in the city and the state were indicted. Of the 10,000 gallons of booze seized, nearly 7,000 gallons were housed at the US Customs and Post Office in Mobile.

Back then, this stately Italianate and Classical Revival structure stood at the corner of Royal and St. Francis Streets. Tragically, as were many iconic Mobile structures in the 1960s, the original building was destroyed in 1964; however, it was also during the 1960s that a plethora of tunnels and secret basements were discovered throughout downtown Mobile; the secret life of many buildings as speakeasys emerged, including today's Alchemy Tavern, which connected to a brothel (now the Haunted Bookshop, which connects to the modern tavern via

### LAS FLORIDITAS

**What:** Cuban-inspired speakeasy

**Where:** 107 St. Francis St.

**Cost:** Varies

**Pro Tip:** You have to have the password to get in. The password is posted on Instagram (@lasfloriditas) every day at noon in bold italic font.

Las Floriditas pays homage to
Lost Generation literary pioneer,
modernist Ernest Hemingway.
The Hemingway Daquiri is a
must try.

a wardrobe-style passage, like the one leading to Narnia), and the Lupercalia Art Society gallery basement.

Today, the speakeasy culture—and Mobile's Cuban connection—of yesteryear is preserved in the same building where liquor from the epic rum-runner raid was stowed almost 100 years ago at Las Floriditas, a Cuban-themed restaurant that is accessible only via password through the now defunct bank vault in the RSA Bank Trust Building's basement. The irony is almost as delicious as the cocktails.

Locals helping federal agents ferret out drinkers and bootleggers would taste drinks they ordered to confirm if the beverage was alcohol, a practice that often eliminated physical evidence.

# THE MALAGA INN

## What were the secret tunnels under the hotel used for?

The Malaga Inn, like most things in Mobile, isn't all that it appears to be. From the outside, it appears to be a charming, historic boutique hotel outfitted with 39 rooms, many of which are full of furnishings original to the home. Of course, it is that.

It also looks like a hotel that's primely located on the corner of Church Street on the main Mardi Gras parade route . . . and it's that, too . . . but, there's a little more to it.

The Malaga was originally a pair of twin homes built by two Bavarian business partners, Isaac Goldsmith and William Frohlichstein, in 1862. The homes served as wedding gifts for the sisters whom these gentlemen had fallen in love with and married.

The homes stayed in the families for years but were eventually sold. In the 1960s, Mayme Sinclair purchased both homes and turned it into the family-run inn that exists today. The Carriage House, now used for weddings, served as a bar and restaurant called Mayme's for a period. Prior to that, it was Octavia's Restaurant and Lounge Club, named for the charming socialite, writer, and abolitionist Octavia Le Vert.

It's suggested the suite above the lobby, where Mayme resided, is haunted. The chandeliers reportedly shake without prompting. Other haunting reports claim a woman dressed in white can sometimes be seen trolling the balcony outside room

### MALAGA INN

**What:** Haunted, historic boutique hotel

**Where:** 359 Church St.

**Cost:** Variable, but typically $89/night for standard room; $179/night for a suite

**Pro Tip:** Accommodations for rooms at the Malaga during Mardi Gras book years in advance.

*Guests of the historic Malaga Inn are given complimentary tours upon availability.*

#007. Presumably, the Malaga ghosts are friendly, as everyone has a great time.

One of the most intriguing secrets of the historic hotel is the tunnels. Under the stairs is a false wall. Inside of the room the wall conceals is a trapdoor in the floor. The narrow passageway leads to a stone tunnel underneath the house. It's believed the tunnel was used to smuggle things and to hide people during the Civil War.

---

Octavia Le Vert had mixed feelings about secession and slavery. Mobilians considered the new widow a traitor when she entertained occupying Union soldiers in her home following the Civil War.

# RIGHT UP AUTOMOTIVE ALLEY

## What's the social scene at the Automotive Alley revival like?

Between fires—lots and lots of fires—economic upheaval, wars, yellow fever, and Prohibition, Mobile's economy has taken a lot of hits. In the 1920s, right before economic times took a notable downward turn, Mobile's Automobile Alley was primed to take advantage of people's rampantly growing needs for personal vehicles.

Located on St. Louis Street in downtown Mobile, the district, unlike Dauphin Street a couple of blocks away, had wide lanes—big enough for cars to drive and to park alongside the road. The whole of St. Louis Street, which is just outside the De Tonti Square Historic District, was populated with car dealerships, a service station, an auto parts store, and other businesses.

It would take over 100 years for the area to pick up again, but the revival is spectacular, as the former automotive buildings have been repurposed into apartment buildings; a Greer's market; the Cheese Cottage; the Wheeler Building, which boasts offices and residential space; Braided River Brewing; Old Majestic Brewing Company; Innovation PortAL; the Buick Building; Olde Mobile Antiques; Fowler Lighting; and more to come. It's one of the most livable areas in downtown Mobile.

Todd Duren's Secret History Tours take visitors on a walk down Automotive Alley with stops at breweries along the way. Other tours focus on local color, history, and ghost stories.

*While Braided River's Summer Crush is worth running for during the week, a lazy Sunday afternoon at the Cheese Cottage is the weekend we're all working for.*

What makes this area particularly desirable is that there's a hub of activity. Old Majestic is always hosting events inside the spacious brewery or on the expansive front lawn. The first-Sunday market each month brings in local artists and artisanal goods, craft vendors, live music, and more. On Wednesday evenings, a running group meets to jog a 5K around downtown. Runners, often the same group, convene on Thursdays at Braided River for similar camaraderie.

It's the perfect setting for a rapidly reviving city. Unlike the 1960s, when urban renewal merited tearing down what already existed, Mobilians are repurposing existing space.

# SWINGING FOR THE FENCES

### Who's arguably the best baseball player in history?

Alabama is best known for football (cue someone shouting "roll tide!"), and with the University of South Alabama Jaguars working their own gridiron, it's only a matter of time before that legacy grows even more prominent; however, it's arguable that the ultimate MVP from Mobile will always be baseball legend Hank Aaron.

Henry "Hank" Aaron was born in 1934 in an area near Magnolia Cemetery called Down the Bay (this is also where the families who served the Ropers lived after the Civil War). The family moved to a home that Aaron's dad, Herbert, built in Toulminville in 1942.

Aaron's first pro-ball job was with the Mobile Black Bears. He played shortstop; less than a decade later, he'd be in the major leagues, having been named MVP in 1957, the same year he hit a home run in the World Series. In 1965, Aaron's younger brother, first baseman Tommie Aaron, would hit the first home-park home run for the Braves; however, nothing outshines Hank Aaron's legacy.

Aaron beat Babe Ruth's 714 home run record with 755 home runs. Other Mobile ball players like Satchel Paige, Ozzie

---

Few will know this but, in 1940, the Alabama Crimson Tide played Spring Hill College on Murphy High School's football field. Few will doubt this, but Alabama won.

*The Hank Aaron Childhood Home and Museum was relocated to the location of the Hank Aaron Stadium. It opened in 2010; tours are available weekdays and on home game days.*

Smith, Willie McCovey, and Billy Williams would all be inducted into the Baseball Hall of Fame.

Today, as noted, football is a bigger beast, but it's still possible to walk and even throw a ball on a field where both Hank Aaron and Babe Ruth played—Stan Galle Field on the Spring Hill College campus. It's the oldest continually used baseball field in the country, and it's a beautiful space to play out those lingering sandlot fantasies.

# HANK AARON CHILDHOOD HOME AND MUSEUM

**What:** Relocated Toulminville childhood home of baseball legend Hank Aaron

**Where:** 755 Bolling Brothers Blvd.

**Cost:** $5 adults, $4 children 12 and under (free admission with a game ticket)

**Pro Tip:** The Hank Aaron Childhood Home and Museum has been voted one of the best baseball museums in the country.

# THE BATTLE HOUSE BRIDE

## Why is the Battle House Mobile's most famous hotel?

The historic Battle House Hotel is famous for many reasons. Though in its original location, it's burned down more than once. It was last rebuilt in 1908 following a 1905 incineration.

Like many old Mobile structures, the Battle House is allegedly haunted. In 1910, a newlywed and her husband were staying at the Battle House. During their visit, the husband was called away on business. As days passed and she waited, hotel staff began to question when she'd be departing. With no word from her husband, the bride despaired. Unable to tolerate the shame of being abandoned, she hanged herself on the Crystal Ballroom chandelier.

It's believed her husband did return. One modern bride reported that she and her mother walked in on a man staring at her wedding portrait. The man quickly vanished and wasn't seen again. It's suspected to be the ghost of the husband wandering the Battle House in hopes of finding his bride.

Another story is of the "honor killing." A former Mardi Gras king, Henry Butler, was caught in a tryst with his queen, Mrs. Raymond Dyson. When the Dyson brothers learned of the dalliance, they lured Butler to room 552 and beat him. They left to call a lawyer to prosecute Butler for his salacious crime, but when hotel staff went to check on Butler, he was dead.

---

Irish humorist Oscar Wilde stayed at the Battle House during a visit in 1882 when he was performing in Mobile.

*At the historic Battle House, if you whisper into the "whisper wall" on the second floor near the main entrance, a person on the other side of the wall can clearly hear what you're saying.*

The fifth floor, where Butler was murdered, is the hotel's most haunted. Reports of other ghosts randomly turning on water spigots and pushing nails out of walls while the Battle House underwent renovations in the 2000s are widespread among Mobilians who know. But these are just stories; you really have to stay and see for yourself.

## THE BATTLE HOUSE RENAISSANCE MOBILE HOTEL AND SPA

**What:** A historic haunted hotel

**Where:** 26 N Royal St.

**Cost:** $279 per night (depending on time of year)

**Pro Tip:** Schedule a spa service and take a dip in the rooftop pool when you visit.

# HAUNTED HOUSE IN DE TONTI

## Who are the children at the Richards-DAR House?

The De Tonti Square Historic District, named after Italian explorer Henri de Tonti, the man with the iron hand (literally), comprises townhomes of Federal, Greek, and Italianate architectural styles. While most structures canopied by towering live oak trees are private homes or businesses, the Richards-DAR House on Joachim is a museum occupied by the Daughters of the American Revolution (DAR) organization.

Once, though, the Italianate townhome was a private residence built for the Richards family in the 1860s. Captain Charles Richards, a steamboat captain from Maine, hoped to live there with his wife, Caroline; however, Caroline died giving birth to the couple's 11th child. Captain Richards spent the next 30 years as a widower, and the home remained in the Richards family for four generations until it was sold in 1946 to the Ideal Cement Company.

In 1973, DAR moved in and realized that the house—though still in pristine original condition—was not entirely unoccupied. It's possible to hear the unmistakable pitter-patter of children's feet racing around on the home's second floor or even on the stairs.

Despite thorough checks of the home, no one living has ever been found hiding out, making a stir.

---

### RICHARDS-DAR HOUSE MUSEUM

**What:** Historic period home and museum that's allegedly haunted

**Where:** 256 N Joachim St.

**Cost:** $10 adults, $5 children ages 5–12

**Pro Tip:** The only tours are Saturday 10–4 and Sundays 1–4; make a weekend of it and pay a visit to nearby Iron Hand Brewing after the tour.

*The Richards-DAR House is characterized by lace ironworks, chandeliers, Carrara marble mantles, and period furnishings.*

Other times, indecipherable whispers can be heard during opening. It's as if the ghosts of the Richards children come out to play at night. Given that five of the Richards children died in childhood, it's a plausible theory, but as they say . . . there's only one way to find out.

Author Augusta Evans briefly lived at 255 State St. It's a distinct, privately owned historic garden home because of the brick wall and arched gate leading to the courtyard.

# PIRATE'S HONEY

## What hotel has a colony of bees on the roof?

Confederate Admiral Raphael Semmes has a long and interesting history—some regard him as a Civil War hero, while others consider the Confederate commerce raider a pirate (and if you've read any of the press about how the victims of his maritime exploits felt, you'll likely lean toward pirate). Whatever the case, the sailor had an illustrious maritime career.

After he retired (barring a brief stint in prison in Washington, DC, in 1865), Semmes returned to practicing law, and when he wasn't bumming around his other home in Josephine, he published books and was a teacher. It was entirely possible for Semmes to fade into obscurity or even to go down in history as a villain of sorts.

Instead, he's largely remembered heroically. This is because of Semmes's daughter. Electra Semmes Colston was the principal at Barton Academy, which opened as a public school in 1852 but was closed briefly for the Civil War. Electra wasn't just the principal, she was also a great PR person who ran a one-woman campaign glorifying her father.

Because of her position and influence, the stories of Semmes's military activities took on a positive slant.

Hence the many nods to Semmes in and around Mobile, like the Admiral, an Art Deco–style hotel opened in 1940.

Its name notwithstanding, the Admiral has little to do with Semmes. In fact, this pet-friendly hotel is a study in refinement,

## THE ADMIRAL

**What:** Hotel with bees on the roof

**Where:** 251 Government St.

**Cost:** Average $219 per night

**Pro Tip:** Pick up a jar of honey at Corner 251; it's made from the bees colonized in the rooftop herb garden.

*Corner 251 was once one of Jimmy Buffett's favorite places to hang out and grab a bite.*

culture, and charm. The most enticing aspect is the rooftop bee colony and herb garden. Honey sourced from the bees and the fresh herbs are used in the dishes and cocktails served at the hotel's Corner 251 restaurant and a charming corner bar. It's certainly something to buzz about.

Josephine is known as a place where pirates liked to hang out. Local pirates were the inspiration for the best-kept-secret haunt nestled in Robert's Bayou, a place Semmes frequented.

# TASTE OF HEAVEN

## Where can I get a sinfully delicious treat with no guilt?

Mobile is home to a plethora of incredible bakeries, but only one sweet in town is free of sin.

The Visitation Monastery on Spring Hill Avenue was established in 1833 by Bishop Michael Porter and spent some time as both a convent and an all-girl's academy. The academy at this historic facility closed in 1952, and the Visitation Shop now occupies the former rectory built in 1899.

Today, the convent, which is a papal cloister, emphasizes peace, prayer, charity, gentleness, and self-control. Approximately 20+ black-habit-donning nuns live at the monastery on Spring Hill Avenue and occupy themselves in days of prayer and pleasant occupation.

In addition to daily morning Mass, the monastery offers retreats—many Mobile Catholics can attest to having started married lives with a memorable Engaged Encounter weekend at the monastery. The retreats and the proceeds from the Visitation Shop, along with donations, fund the monastery.

The Visitation Shop has books, prayer cards, christening gowns, and, oh yes . . . "heavenly hash." The handmade sweet treat is made of marshmallow, chocolate, and pecans. Starting in 2000, Sister Theodosia has overseen the process of making heavenly hash. It takes days to produce. The hash is produced in increasing quantities during Christmas, when it sells the most. The hash is sold in half-pound and one-pound boxes, and

---

The Convent of Mercy was built in 1908 at 753 St. Francis St. and is Mobile's only other surviving historic convent. In 2002, the building became St. Francis Place Condominiums.

*Many believe that one has to be Catholic to visit the monastery or to pray; however, such is not the case.*

they literally sell thousands of pounds each holiday season. The nuns who make the treat do so as a labor of love, for that's the essence of their cloister.

## VISITATION MONASTERY

**What:** The closest you'll get to heaven in Mobile

**Where:** 2300 Springhill Ave.

**Cost:** $14.50/pound or $8/half pound

**Pro Tip:** Come with an eye for the obscure. In addition to the hash, the Visitation Shop carries a wealth of ever-changing oddities.

# IT'S GOOD TO BE GREEK

## What's the sweetest spot in town?

Mobilians look forward to Greek Fest every fall the same way they look forward to Mardi Gras, azaleas blooming, and a break in summer's blazing heat. Greek Fest is a four-day affair of dining, dancing, drinking, and shopping—a veritable immersion in all that is Greek—that started in Mobile in 1962.

Of course, the Greek descendance to Mobile started far before that. The Greeks were among the many immigrant groups to come to Mobile (the largest were the Irish fleeing the potato famine). Greeks came in the late 1800s to escape the Ottoman Empire.

With no connections to lean on, most of the Greek immigrants gravitated toward the food industry, for which we are all eternally grateful. They were fish sellers and candy and nut makers. Like most cultural groups, Mobile's new Greek community was bound by their shared experiences and beliefs. Many were just trying to survive, sending money home to help others escape.

While many of the businesses established have since shuttered (such as the popular Constantine's and Rousseau's on the Causeway), one has survived over a century. Three Georges, a candy and nut shop, was established in 1917 by three Greek Georges—Pappolamporous (Pappas), Coudopolos, and Sparr.

The business, housed in a mint-green ("cerulean blue," according to Eugene Walter) building built in 1866, uses the

## THREE GEORGES

**What:** Classic candy shop and soda fountain started by three Greek Georges

**Where:** 226 Dauphin St.

**Cost:** $5–$75; products range from individual chocolates to gift baskets and cakes

**Pro Tip:** Pick up a pack of cheese straws while you're in the shop; it's one of their best-kept (and most delicious) secrets.

*Three Georges sits at the popular corner of Dauphin and Joachim Streets and has delighted children of all ages with its confections and savories for generations.*

same equipment and the same recipes handwritten by Pappas over a century ago.

In 1992, Euple, Pappas's widow, sold the shop but stayed close by to ensure things were done properly. This level of attentive care reflects how the Greeks were able to thrive and eventually establish the Greek Orthodox Brotherhood and the Greek Church of the Annunciation in Mobile, which is where the Greek culture thrives and, once a year, Greek Fest takes place.

Jason Malbis, one of the first Grecian immigrants in 1869, helped many locals get established and even owned Malbis Bakery, which was later bought by Smith's Bakery, in downtown Mobile.

# MIDDLE BAY MOO HOUSE

## Why did a cow live on a lighthouse in the middle of the bay?

The Middle Bay Lighthouse, activated in 1885, is in the middle of Mobile Bay between the Eastern Shore and downtown Mobile . . . hence the name.

The lighthouse was constructed to aid ships making their way through the newly dredged Mobile Bay to the Port of Mobile; without the lighthouse, there wasn't enough visibility on the 29-mile route, making it otherwise dangerous.

For years, the hexagonal lighthouse located in the middle of the bay was manned by a series of keepers and those keepers' families (if they had them). Each keeper lived on the lighthouse. Quite spectacularly, in 1916, the lighthouse keeper and his wife had a baby; however, the new mother was unable to nurse her infant, and something had to be done.

The lighthouse keeper built a small corral on the lighthouse gallery and then went to town and procured a milking cow, which he then brought to the lighthouse to provide the necessary milk for his baby. Each week, the man returned to shore for supplies and hay to feed the cow.

The cow's tenure at the lighthouse was brief. On July 5, 1916, a powerful hurricane swept into Mobile Bay bringing 11'6"-foot

Visitors are no longer allowed to walk onto the historic lighthouse; however, the unique shape and style of the structure make it well worth taking the guided tour which features the lighthouse and other areas of Mobile Bay.

*Private boaters and bar pilots use the iconic lighthouse as a navigational point.*

storm surges, the highest ever reported in Mobile. The little family and their cow escaped in the nick of time. The lighthouse survived but was damaged and had to undergo repairs.

In 1935, the lighthouse was automated, and by the 1960s it had fallen into disrepair. When it was deactivated in 1967, some wanted to destroy it. It was argued, though, that the lighthouse was still useful, as ship radars could detect it and use it as a reference point as they came in and out of port.

In the 2000s, the lighthouse was refurbished. It now serves as a Dauphin Island Sea Lab Weather Station and provides real-time maritime information.

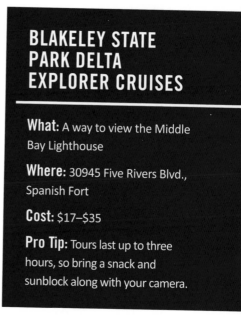

## BLAKELEY STATE PARK DELTA EXPLORER CRUISES

**What:** A way to view the Middle Bay Lighthouse

**Where:** 30945 Five Rivers Blvd., Spanish Fort

**Cost:** $17–$35

**Pro Tip:** Tours last up to three hours, so bring a snack and sunblock along with your camera.

# THE HERMIT OF GOAT ISLAND

### Was there really a guy who lived on Goat Island?

Once upon a time, there lived a man named Peter Bernard. "Pete" was a regular guy who settled down only to realize family life wasn't for him. He's described as a "drifter" who moved away from his Wisconsin home to make a living as a shipbuilder.

Pete wandered to Mobile in 1910 and got a job in the shipyard. Pete sent part of his earnings home to his family. Eventually, Pete made his way back home, but his family was gone—Pete had no way to reach them.

Pete thus returned to Mobile and continued building ships. He was so efficient he was nicknamed "Battleship Pete." When Battleship Pete retired, he opened a waterfront tavern called the Oyster Bar, a place for tossing back suds and playing rounds of poker.

One day, a photographer snapped a photo of Pete in a poker game at the CIO Hall. The image, which appeared in the *Shipbuilder* magazine, was discovered by Peter Bernard Jr., Battleship Pete's son who'd been searching for his father for 40 years. Peter Jr. soon reunited grandly with his long-lost father at the Oyster Bar. Two years later, Pete's 87-year-old sister traveled from California to reconnect with Pete.

---

## THE HUMMINGBIRD WAY OYSTER BAR

**What:** Neighborhood oyster bar in the Oakleigh District

**Where:** 351 George St.

**Cost:** $3 per oyster or $17 for a dozen grilled oyster casino

**Pro Tip:** Hummingbird is a little posher than Pete's tavern, but you get to experience the different flavors of farmed oysters at this local haunt open 5–10 p.m. Tuesday through Saturday.

Top Chef *alum Jim Smith runs a Southern oyster bar not far from Pete's original Royal Street oyster bar.*

Pete was in his 80s when his second wife died. Devastated, he sold the tavern and moved to Little Sand Island on Mobile Bay, which Pete rechristened Goat Island because he allegedly kept goats on the island. Pete's new moniker became "The Hermit of Goat Island."

Despite wanting a quiet retirement, Pete's life was ever a spectacle. When his boat wouldn't run, he was rescued by the Brookley Air Force. Tragically, in 1966, Pete was in town for supplies, something he avoided doing as much as possible because of the hustle and bustle it brought, when he was hit and killed by a car at age 96.

Between 1862 and 1865, the private island where the hermit Battleship Pete took up residence was part of Mobile Bay's Civil War defenses.

# PLANE CRAZY

### What's the seedy, sailor history behind Brookley?

Mobile's oldest industry is—pause for scandal—prostitution. We know that in a city with more churches than Dollar Generals, the notion that prostitution was not only permitted but that it thrived is unfathomable. However, by the early 1800s, saloons, boarding houses, and gambling dens proliferated along the waterfront.

The red-light district started just past Theater Street. Beyond that, around Royal and Water Streets, was a dastardly place called Spanish Alley, a deadly hangout for hard knocks and illicit activities. Being stabbed in the back was a common occurrence. One saloon, the Bloody Barrel, was so dangerous you weren't likely to come out alive if you dared enter. Despite this, it's documented that folks in Spanish Alley attended Sunday Mass as faithfully as they did the seedy saloons. In 1873, Spanish Alley caught fire and burned, and it wasn't rebuilt (fancy that).

Instead, it was refashioned for railway, as Mobile was in a period of prosperous growth. The Mobile waterfront bustled with parks reminiscent of Coney Island. Where today's railways, interstate, convention center, and Brookley Field are were Monroe and Arlington Parks, a continuous roadway called Bay Shell Road, the original Mobile Country Club, fairgrounds, Crystal Pool, a carousel, horse racing, and more.

Tragically, a series of hurricanes from 1906–1926 devastated the waterfront, and much of what was there

In 1721, 17 years after the Pelican Girls landed, Parisian prostitutes arrived from a French prison to marry settlers. Many believe the Pelican Girls were also prostitutes. They weren't.

*Regina's used to be located at Fort Condé, so it's always been a venue for welcoming people to Mobile.*

was moved inland. Bates Field became the Mobile airport, which permanently divided the continuous bayfront road.

World War II and the US military's need for the space pushed Bates Field out west. In the '60s, the military returned Brookley Field to Mobile, which left it basically defunct until aerospace-industry investment picked up in the '90s and '00s. A modern-day urban renewal has finally brought the commercial airport back to Brookley. In summer 2024, Brookley will officially be the site of Mobile Downtown Airport (BFM).

## REGINA'S KITCHEN

**What:** Sandwich shop at Brookley Aerocomplex

**Where:** 1801 15th St.

**Cost:** $7.50–$15

**Pro Tip:** Arrive early to this lunch spot, which is only open from 11 a.m. to 2 p.m. The Schoel is their most popular sandwich.

# THE MIGHTY A

## How did the battleship get to Mobile Bay?

The USS *Alabama*, a BB-60 battleship built in Norfolk in 1940, is an unmistakable sight as you pull out of the Bankhead Tunnel and onto the Causeway. The ship sits in Battleship Memorial Park alongside a submarine and several other military planes and jets.

Also known simply as "the Battleship," the USS *Alabama* was the largest ever built in Portsmouth, Virginia, weighing a striking 35,000 tons (45,000 when loaded). It was designed to be one of the fastest, and when at sea in the Pacific it was instrumental in taking Japanese islands during World War II.

Despite serving 37 casualty-free months—a feat that earned the ship the moniker "the Mighty A," the ship was set to be scrapped by the US Navy following World War II in the spring of 1962.

Alabamians weren't having it and instead asked if they could bring the ship home to Mobile Bay to serve as a memorial for all the Alabamians who'd given their lives in service to the US.

An agreement was penned, and the state of Alabama collectively began fundraising with the most remarkable contribution being from schoolchildren. The local children turned in dimes, nickels, and quarters to raise a remarkable $100,000 to go toward the ship's three-month trek to bring it to Mobile in 1964.

---

Each November, runners start on Old Spanish Trail and run a 12K to Battleship Memorial Park that finishes at the USS *Alabama* in honor of and gratitude to veterans.

*With 129 guns and three 16-inch 45-caliber guns capable of shooting a target 20 miles away, the battleship was designed for shore bombardment and antiaircraft defense.*

The USS *Alabama*, which bears a width of 108 feet, squeezed through the Panama Canal (it literally had only 11 inches to spare on either side).

The ship is now a popular tourism draw. Not only are there many events, including July 4 fireworks and a kite day hosted at the Battleship Memorial Park each year, but many movies, including *Under Siege* (1992) with Steven Seagal, Gary Busey, and Tommy Lee Jones and *USS Indianapolis: Men of Courage* (2016) with Nicolas Cage and Tom Sizemore, have used the USS *Alabama* as a setting.

## USS *ALABAMA*

**What:** World War II battleship

**Where:** 2703 Battleship Pkwy.

**Cost:** $5 parking + $6–$18 general admission

**Pro Tip:** Every other month, historical reenactors demonstrate what wartime life was like aboard the ship.

# THE CANNON

## What's the story of the cannon at Memorial Park?

Located on a triangular thatch of grass at "the Loop," Memorial Park observes a steady flow of traffic on all sides, making it easy to overlook. Such wasn't the case in 1926, though, when the park was established by the Mother's Army and Navy League. Back then, the Loop was where the trolley circled around before heading back downtown, and where the Sylacauga marble monument displaying the 63 names of Mobilians who died in World War I was noticed by all.

Today, it's the cannon that catches people's eye. Ironically, the cannon has nothing to do with World War I or Mobile. Rather, it's a Civil War relic likely donated by the US after the war. Until it was moved to its current location in 1953 when the Bankhead Tunnel was built, it occupied space on Government Street near a sister cannon.

Ironically, in addition to serving as a point of reference ("turn at the cannon"), the cannon also serves as a trophy in a local gridiron civil war. Murphy High School, a historic Spanish-roof-tile complex of structures once considered the most beautiful institution in the state, located a few blocks away on Carlen Street, battles for "ownership" of the cannon against McGill High School, the Catholic school that was Jimmy Buffett's alma mater, located a few blocks away. If McGill wins, the cannon is painted orange; if Murphy wins, it's blue.

---

Until his death in 2005, adored local Lamar Wilson (the Peanut Man) would sell A&M Peanut Shop peanuts at the cannon. He did this for 40 years.

*Mobile Mardi Gras's purple and gold stand for justice and power. Green (faith) was adopted by New Orleans in 1872 in honor of Grand Duke Alexis Alexandrovich Romanov.*

It's a time-honored tradition. The cannon also turns pink for breast cancer awareness, and this year, it was painted purple and gold in honor of Mobile Mardi Gras by the 2001 Murphy High School alum Andy Scott, who owns New Hand Signs.

Most of the time, the cannon is painted black (slimming, goes with everything . . . makes sense), but it's a noticeable feature and landmark and is one worth knowing a few secrets about.

## THE CANNON

**What:** Civil War cannon at a WWI memorial

**Where:** Houston and Old Government Streets

**Cost:** Free

**Pro Tip:** The cannon weighs 16,000 pounds, and it's a crime to vandalize it. Taking photos is perfectly fine.

# FLOWER POWER

## How do they keep the flowers in bloom at Bellingrath?

Bellingrath Gardens and Home has a rich and widely known history—many know the 65-acre estate was originally a fish camp owned and established by Walter and Bessie Bellingrath, Mobile's first Coca-Cola bottler. The gardens were created at the camp in the 1920s, and in 1932 Walter ran an ad in the paper offering anyone who'd like to come see the spring garden while in bloom the chance to do so free of charge. The viewing was a hit, and in 1934 they kept the gardens tour opened throughout the year.

Like the flowers that grew there, the gardens bloomed with several prominent displays throughout the year—tulips, mums, azaleas, Christmas lights. While Mobile has a hospitable climate for the flowers, more goes into making the floral displays possible.

Few know that the tulips have to be forced into growing at just the right time. The bulbs arrive from Holland each fall and are immediately chilled at 35 degrees for up to 16 weeks. In January, the bulbs are transplanted to cool greenhouses, where they begin to bud. Once they bud, they're transferred to the gardens, where they bloom for the delight of guests.

This process is repeated every two weeks, which allows for a two-month blooming period of tulips and other colorful, springy blooms (like hyacinths and daffodils) rather than their normal life cycle of two weeks.

### BELLINGRATH GARDENS AND HOME

**What:** Mobile's largest historic garden attraction

**Where:** 12401 Bellingrath Gardens Rd., Theodore

**Cost:** $8–14 for gardens only; $14–$22 for gardens and home; kids 4 and under are free

**Pro Tip:** Try to visit during December for the epic Magic Christmas in Lights display; it's one of the best holiday events on the Gulf Coast.

*The late "Doc" Brown, who managed Bellingrath until 1993, referenced gardens he'd seen in Japan during WWII and the Korean War when designing the Asian-American Garden. Image credit: Bellingrath Gardens and Home*

Maintaining the gardens is a full-time job; the general manager typically resides on the property in a house on Fowl River built in the 1950s. Tending the gardens, especially during inclement weather, is a full-time job, but it's rewarding, as evidenced by the tireless dedication of those who run the gardens, the home, and the Magnolia Café, which serves a rotating lunch menu.

Hurricane Frederic destroyed 90 percent of the gardens in 1979; 2,400 trees were uprooted or destroyed. It took nearly six months to clear away debris and revive the gardens.

# 21ST-CENTURY THEATER

## What's Mobile's oldest independent theater?

Even though Netflix and Amazon Prime and other digital platforms have largely taken over entertainment, people in Mobile still go to the movies. The Crescent Theater on Dauphin Street was opened in 2008, but before it was a movie theater . . . it was a movie theater. In fact, this little stretch of Dauphin Street boasted several theaters at one point.

The building was constructed in 1885 but didn't become the Century Theatre until 1936. Designed by Mobile legacy Cooper Van Antwerp, the theater was a stunning example of Art Moderne décor and architecture. Art Moderne is a style born from Art Deco. Just two doors down from this theater was the Beaux Arts–informed Empire Theatre, which was tragically leveled after its early 1960s closure to make a parking lot.

### THE CRESCENT THEATER

**What:** An independent movie theater located in a historic building

**Where:** 208 Dauphin St.

**Cost:** $12 per ticket

**Pro Tip:** Arrive early and enjoy appetizers at the Noble South, the former Bijou, before your show.

The Bijou was no longer listed after 1932, but the building still stands. Farm-to-table casual fine dining restaurant the Noble South now occupies the old theater's space.

*The Crescent Theater features a combination of independent films, local cinema, national and international films, and live performances.*

Across the street at 205 Dauphin was the Bijou Theatre, a former silent theater (the Bijou was previously named the Majestic and the Dauphine). Dauphin Street's theaters shuttered as Mobilians moved to the suburbia of West Mobile, where larger cineplexes populated.

The Century Theatre lay dormant from the time it closed in 1964 to the time it burned (a rite of passage for Mobile architecture, if you think about it) in 2004. It was heavily remodeled and serves as a thriving independent movie theater today. It was the only theater (excluding the Saenger off Joachim Street) to survive as a movie theater.

# THE SHOW MUST GO ON

## Why was the "Jewel of Joachim" almost destroyed?

Today's downtown Mobile reflects urban revivalism with new small businesses, local breweries, murals, diners, and more popping up and paying homage to Mobile's history (for example, Braided River is thusly named for the network of rivers that flow into the delta).

The 61st Saenger Theatre, Mobile's Saenger, was established in 1927, the work of J. D. and A. H. Saenger, who founded their first theater in New Orleans. Other theaters appeared around the South, the Caribbean, and Mexico.

The palatial theater's decor incorporates elements of Greek mythology; images of Poseidon, Dionysus, and Pan are prominent in the theater's grand entrance, which features gilded finishes, trompe l'oeil decoration, and a marble staircase winding up to the mezzanine. Crystal chandeliers and other elegant furnishings are inspired by European opera houses.

For years, the Saenger hosted vaudeville, cinema, and live theater; it was also the setting for America's first Junior Miss pageant. Despite its success, due to the cost of maintaining the venue, along with probable declining patronage thanks to the western migration during the 1960s' urban renewal period, the owner, ABC/Paramount, was ready to see it destroyed.

Then, the night before the theater's demise, the University of South Alabama swooped in and purchased the Saenger, rescuing it from destruction. Today, the Saenger, now owned by

---

Before it was the Saenger, the historic Joachim Street building housed Three Georges, a Greek-owned candy shop now housed less than a block away.

*It cost $500,000 to build the Saenger in 1927; today that cost would be $7.6 million.*

the City of Mobile and operated by the Center for the Living Arts, is a thriving performing arts center and is home to the Mobile Symphony Orchestra.

With such an eclectic history, the Saenger fits right in on Joachim Street, where on one end there's a German-American restaurant and a Greek-owned confectionary and on the other a brothel turned bookshop and a gay bar with ties to Prohibition. Ongoing art exhibitions at the neighboring Mobile Arts Council and shows at the theater keep the theater's lights as bright as its future.

## SAENGER THEATRE

**What:** Historic theater and home to Mobile Symphony Orchestra

**Where:** 6 S Joachim St.

**Cost:** Variable (depending on show)

**Pro Tip:** The theater backs up to Cathedral Square and is the best place to get an autograph after a show.

# MEAL FIT FOR A KING

## What was Elvis's favorite restaurant in Mobile?

Everybody has at least one Elvis story. This is ours. Back in the mid-'50s, before Elvis was . . . you know, Elvis . . . he was just a musician struggling to make it. In May 1955, he played a show at Ladd-Peebles Stadium along with 25 other artists for $1. Even though he wasn't the King of Rock and Roll, the handsome crooner inspired teenage girls to chase him across the stadium's football field.

He'd perform in Mobile again in 1955 at the Vigor High School auditorium. The principal pulled the curtains after half an hour because of Elvis's style of dancing (what a hound dog). He also had two other shows during that time.

One was held at the massive music hall the Curtis Gordon's Radio Ranch Club off Cedar Point Road on Dauphin Island Parkway. The other took place at the Greater Gulf State Fairgrounds in Prichard. By the '70s, he was booking at Municipal Auditorium, known today as the Civic Center.

During his many visits, Elvis was known to dine at the Bluegill off the Causeway in Spanish Fort. He sat in the same

Allegedly, probably in the '50s, Elvis slept on the couch at the WMOB AM radio station. Others report he stayed in room 116 of the Causeway's now-demolished "old pink hotel."

Established in 1958, the Bluegill is the ultimate local dive bar with a huge back deck overlooking the bay and frequent live music. More cowbell!

booth, #24, on each of his visits. While the booth is no longer there, there's a plaque and a cardboard cutout of Elvis elsewhere in the restaurant.

By the '70s, Elvis's star had risen so high that he was booking at Municipal Auditorium. During his visits when he was world famous, Elvis would book a suite at the Admiral Semmes Hotel and enjoy room service hamburgers, chips, and champagne. It's different, but it sounds fun.

# COOKIE-CUTTER HOME

## Where can I stay in a home ordered from a catalog?

You can't miss the massive Queen Anne mansion on Monterey Street in midtown Mobile (MiMo); it looks like a little girl's dollhouse all grown up. The house was once owned by Mobile educator Kate Shepard and came from a kit purchased through a mail-order catalog (this was before Sears, Roebuck, and Co. sold Sears Modern Homes in their catalog).

The home was built in 1897 by Kate, who was then principal of the Spring Hill School. In 1910, Kate and her sister Isabel opened the Misses Shepard School and Kindergarten. They lived there with their brother Charles, who was the "head of household."

When Kate passed away in 1952, the school closed. Isabel died a year later. The house was converted into a bed-and-breakfast by subsequent owners, and while the aesthetics and the historical artifacts such as three stained-glass windows are enticing enough, the house is also reportedly haunted, making it a huge source of interest for ghost hunters.

**THE KATE SHEPARD HOUSE**

**What:** A mail-order historic house that is a popular BNB

**Where:** 1552 Monterey Pl.

**Cost:** Average $175 per night

**Pro Tip:** Spend time perusing the historic artifacts and old papers found in the attic; Kate's McRae relatives were Civil War generals.

The spinster sisters are interred together at the historic Magnolia Cemetery located on Virginia Street in Square 11, Lot 29.

*The 4,200-square-foot Kate Shepard House was shipped from Knoxville to Mobile via train. The kit required 13 boxcars to make the journey.*

People often talk about the little girl who lives in the home, which is odd, since none of the Shepard siblings had children. It forces the question . . . what happened here to lead a child to never leave? The ghost is allegedly mischievous and moves things around, playing pranks on guests and the owner.

Maybe the ghost just doesn't like people knowing old family recipes, which were found among papers left in the house. The B&B's pecan praline French toast, the recipe for which is shared on the home's blog, is as legendary as the house it's served in. Tuck in.

# CHEESEBURGER IN PARADISE

## Where can I get Jimmy Buffett's favorite cheeseburger?

Jimmy Buffett's laid-back island-style country music conveys that the crooner was born in a coconut on a sandy beach in Key West and spent his days perfecting the art of strumming the guitar from the comfort of a hammock. Not so.

In fact, Jimmy Buffett was born in Pascagoula, Mississippi, a town less than an hour's drive from Mobile. Because his parents aspired for Buffett to become a Jesuit priest or a naval officer, they enrolled him in Catholic schools in Mobile (and, like any good Catholic, he failed their ambitions spectacularly).

Buffett was both a Boy Scout and an altar boy at St. Ignatius. His schooling was completed at the then all-boy's school, McGill Institute (now McGill Toolen). While he wouldn't learn to play the guitar until he started his undergraduate studies at Auburn (it was, he believed, the best way to meet girls), he did invest much of his free time in leisure hobbies popular along the Gulf Coast: boating, fishing, swimming . . . you get the idea.

Just up Old Shell Road from Buffett's high school is the restaurant billed as Mobile's oldest, Dew Drop Inn. Established in 1924, Dew Drop would've been a hopping spot for the teens in

Though Buffett's cheeseburger lust was formed at Mobile's Dew Drop Inn, "Cheeseburger in Paradise" was written after a perilous boat trip to the island of Tortola where Buffett and his starving friends discovered a cheeseburger restaurant "like a mirage" on a dock.

*Dew Drop is famous for their hot dogs, but it's not hard to see what Jimmy loved so much about cheeseburgers.*

Buffett's time (it still is, actually). While the restaurant may be better known for their loaded chili dogs, the cheeseburgers took Buffett's heart.

Buffett wrote that his "burger lust was formulated at the Dew Drop Inn" and calls the burgers the country's best, so if you're wondering where to find one of the paradise-lover's favorite cheeseburgers, look no further. The whereabouts of his shaker of salt are still unknown.

## DEW DROP INN

**What:** Mobile's oldest restaurant

**Where:** 1808 Old Shell Rd.

**Cost:** $10 and under

**Pro Tip:** After lunch, head over to Cammie's Old Dutch for homemade ice cream and have an authentic midtown Mobile high school–style dining experience.

# RENAISSANCE MAN

## Where would Eugene Walter go to get a drink?

Mobile is a veritable gumbo of glitter and ghosts and glory and grit and gumption. It's a city of many cultural influences—the City of 6 Flags—and even more rises and falls. There is no one Mobilian who better epitomizes the city's eclectic lore than Eugene Walter.

Walter was born in Mobile in 1921. A runaway at age three, he was raised by his grandparents until he was orphaned at age 10. Department store heir Hammond Gayfer adopted Walter. Walter lived with Gayfer at his Dog River home and encouraged creativity and the arts. Walter understood the assignment.

Walter absconded to Europe in the 1940s. He was living in Paris by the '50s and worked in the literary arts. Here, Walter helped launch the revered literary magazine the *Paris Review*.

He moved to Italy in the '50s and acted in several productions. He also hosted epic dinner parties attended by notable guests, including Judy Garland, T. S. Eliot, William Faulkner, Gore Vidal, and Richard Wright.

His illustrious film career boasts dozens of acting, production, writing, and soundtrack credits, like the song "What Is a Youth" from the 1968 *Romeo and Juliet* film.

Walter returned to Mobile in 1979. He said, "Sooner or later all Southerners come home, not to die, but to eat gumbo."

Walter's illustrious life ended in Mobile in March 1998. He died penniless, as was the fashion for postmodern expatriates,

## THE HABERDASHER

**What:** Classic cocktail bar (the place Eugene would've gone)

**Where:** 113 Dauphin St.

**Cost:** Varies; approximately $10–$15 for a craft cocktail

**Pro Tip:** Each of the cocktails is made to order.

*Eugene's tombstone fittingly reads, "When all else fails, throw a party." Undoubtedly, his venue of choice for kicking off the festivities would've been the Haberdasher.*

but his friends did him proper with a wake at the Scottish Rite Temple and a jazz funeral leading to the Church Street Graveyard.

Walter's colorful life can easily be viewed as a metaphor for Mobile's rich history and glittering future. Walter was a Renaissance man from a Renaissance city. It's only fitting that once in a while we raise our glasses for Eugene Walter.

Walter attended Murphy High School in the 1930s where he befriended Mary Van Antwerp. Van Antwerp says when Walter returned to Mobile in 1979, he had 17 cats.

# THE HAUNTED BOOK SHOP

## What really haunts the bookshop?

Mobile has a lot of ghosts and hauntings, so it's not a surprise that we have a bookshop called the Haunted Book Shop, but what actually "haunts" the bookshop may come as a bit of a plot twist.

The Haunted Book Shop was founded in 1941 by current owner, author Angela Trigg's grandmother, Adelaide Marson, and Cameron Plummer. Marston eventually sold her stake to the Plummer family, who maintained the Conception Street store until 1991, when it closed.

In 2019, Angela reopened her family's namesake bookshop in what was coincidentally the former location of Bienville Books, an independent bookstore unrelated to the Haunted Book Shop. (Such coincidence only flies in nonfiction.)

In 2022, the Haunted Book Shop relocated to Joachim Street across from the historic Saenger Theatre and adjacent to Alchemy Tavern, a speakeasy turned modern-day music club. The second-floor bookshop has a keen bird's-eye view of the original Conception Street shop.

The Haunted Book Shop carries a highly representative selection of books. A posh coffee bar and tearoom make for the quintessential reader experience. There's even a cat, Mr. Bingley. (Is it even a bookstore if there's not a cat?)

---

**THE HAUNTED BOOK SHOP AND TEA ROOM**

**What:** A hip, locally owned bookstore in downtown Mobile

**Where:** 109 Dauphin St.

**Cost:** Depends on how you feel about books

**Pro Tip:** Mr. Bingley loves a good head scratch.

---

*The Haunted Book Shop & Tea Room has a huge selection of locally and nationally acclaimed works and book-related gifts for word lovers of all ages.*

It will only be when you leave that you understand why the bookshop is called "haunted." No, there aren't any spooky ghosts (that we know of), but those who enter will be haunted by the books they leave behind (cue Vincent Price laughter).

The Haunted Book Shop was named for Christopher Morley's 1919 book of the same name, which states that the eponymous bookshop is ". . . haunted by the ghosts of all great literature." Per Trigg, it's the books that you don't read that haunt you, and as we all know . . . there's only one way to give up the ghost.

In 1913, President Woodrow Wilson vowed to "never again seek an additional foot of territory by conquest" on the corner of Joachim and Conti, just outside where the bookshop now stands.

# THE BAKERY

## Where can I refuel mind, body, and spirit?

With fresh bread readily available in the bakery section of any grocery store, the idea that there used to be several bakeries throughout Mobile may seem a little peculiar. There were a couple on the old waterfront—Yuille's and the Malbis Bakery, to name two—and there was Smith's Bakery that ended up in midtown.

Gordon Smith descended on Mobile from New Orleans in 1899. After he spent a year working as a grocer, he opened his first Smith's Bakery location on Conception Street. He listed the building for sale, but it ended up burning (fires were quite common at the time). Thus, it was in 1902 that he opened the Dauphin Street Smith's Bakery. Nostalgic locals remember watching bread being made through the bakery windows and even being given a warm uncut loaf at the back door at the end of the day.

Following Gordon's passing in the '60s, the family relinquished the business to Bimbo Bakeries USA in 1989, and the Dauphin Street venue shuttered. In 1994, The Bakery Café

Briefly, a restaurant run by Wesley True called True Midtown Kitchen occupied the bakery building. True, a Mobile native, was a contestant on season 13 of *Top Chef*.

*Red or White was the first retail store in the state to incorporate a full menu of exquisite small bites with a drink service.*

opened, reviving the building. The large warehouse served as the dining room and a bar area was built in the Dauphin-facing upper room. Original doors and window treatments remained to preserve the integrity of the original bakery.

Now, the Red or White wine bar, notable for the large selection of vinos and the incredible wood-fired pizzas, occupies the space. Also on site is Kindred Yoga Studio, making it the perfect place to align your chakras and then refuel your body with delicious food and your favorite varietal.

# ICE, ICE, BABY

## Where are the beers cold and the doggies hot?

Before the late 1920s, ice was a costly commodity in Mobile, where humid summer temperatures creep into the 90s. Only a pitcher of heavily iced tea (or iced bourbon with Perrier and a splash of amaretto "for color," as the Southern ladies used to clandestinely sip on) can cool a body down on such a day.

A hundred years ago, though, the ice for said tea would've run you quite the penny. In fact, ice, which was shipped in from the north, was so pricey you probably couldn't have afforded it (brutal). In 1927, all of that changed. The Crystal Ice Factory opened in Mobile off Monroe Street in the Church Street East Historic District, and things quickly cooled off.

As the factory's facilities evolved and ice for personal and commercial use became an increasingly common luxury (shout-out to the modern fridge), the Crystal Ice Factory triumvirate of services—making, storing, and distributing ice—was no longer needed; the buildings were growing derelict as glorified storage spaces, so in 2015 the property was sold to make way for new and exciting things.

In 2019, the distribution building was revived as the Ice Box Bar. Much of the original interior is maintained in homage to the Crystal Ice Factory, so you're literally walking into a giant former freezer for an ice-cold beverage (and during the summer swelter, nothing tastes, looks, or feels better). TVs and pool tables inside and a spacious back deck and patio tables and

In 1933, the night manager and an employee were robbed at pistol point. The thieves stole $12–$13 (roughly $300 in today's money). The investigation is ongoing.

*A frosty cold drink enjoyed inside the Ice Box Bar or outside in the courtyard is peak Southern living.*

swings outside make this dive bar a great place to chill.

Meanwhile, the factory building was converted into HopHounds Brew Pub, Mobile's first dog park, bar, and eatery, in 2020. The massive play yard gives doggies plenty of space to run around while their owners kick back and relax. Ice for your drink is on the house.

## ICE BOX BAR; HOPHOUNDS BREW PUB

**What:** Dive bar and dog playground

**Where:** 755 / 806 Monroe St.

**Cost:** No cost to enter for drinks at either bar; $10 per dog for a day pass to HopHounds

**Pro Tip:** Sticks and Stacks Craft Eatery only serves food at HopHounds on Tuesdays and Fridays through Sundays.

# DIG INTO THE GARAGE

## Where's the best free crawfish in Mobile?

The state of Alabama is home to 97 different species of crawfish. That beats Louisiana and anywhere else for miles. Thus, come spring, crawfish boils abound at bars in downtown Mobile.

Other than not having one, there's no wrong way to do a crawfish boil. You fill a large pot with water, seasoning (lots and lots of seasoning), vegetables (traditionally corn, potatoes, mushrooms, onions . . . your choice . . . pineapple, Brussels sprouts, etc. have been used with great success), sausage (or not, but it makes it better), and, of course, crawfish. A hunk of butter is cool, too.

Crawfish float to the top of the pot once they're cooked, and they're ladled out along with delicious vegetables, which have soaked up all of that incredible richly seasoned flavor into a serving basket or onto a table covered in newspaper. Step two is to put your beer to one side and dig in.

The real question is how to eat crawfish. Some people pinch the back and eat the meat out of the thing, which is fine, but some suck the heads. You want to suck the heads. It's considered the "poor man's foie gras." No, you're not sucking out the late crawfish's brain (it doesn't have one). It's actually a sort of fat pocket (like a liver) that's richly flavored and makes a world of difference in how your crawfish tastes.

**THE GARAGE**

**What:** Historic dive bar in town for free crawfish

**Where:** 9 S Washington Ave.

**Cost:** Free for crawfish; average $3 for a drink

**Pro Tip:** Sunday music is 3–7, but happy hour is noon–4, so show up at around 2 to get the best of both worlds.

*Sundays at the Garage are a favorite pastime for many.*

Now that you know how, you need to know where. There's no better place to go for free crawfish on Sundays in spring than the Garage, a dive bar in downtown Mobile known for killer live music, great happy hours, and wide-open garage bays that lead to the outside and let the whole place fill with the rich smell of free boiled crawfish. It's the most wonderful time of the year.

The Garage was built in 1921 and was a radiator shop. It became a bar in 1994. Back then, the garage doors would open for visitors to park their Harleys.

# CURIOUS COFFEE CULTURE

## Where can I get a cup of coffee and a new facial hairdo?

Back in the 1860s, Italian immigrant Sylvester Festorazzi opened Captain Sylvester Festorazzi's Coffee Saloon at 12 S Royal St. The coffee saloon was known for its coffee, which was parched, ground by hand, and made in volumes of no more than a gallon at a time. Patrons had to be patient, but it was coffee worth waiting for.

Fast-forward to 2022, and the local coffee culture in Mobile is just as discerning—for example, John Serda of Serda's Coffee Company on Royal Street studied abroad in Costa Rica and even opened a wildly successful coffee venture there before returning to Mobile to open his namesake coffee company, which only deals in hand-roasted small-batch coffee.

Just as meticulous is the brewing process at relative newcomer KnuckleBones Elixir Co., part of the Social Experiment, a collective that also includes Beard and Blade barbershop. The shops are housed in a large, Art Deco–inspired shared space that was previously a parking garage.

The mirrors, long bar, and posh decor are inviting, but the process is even more intriguing. At KnuckleBones, a Yama cold brew tower drips coffee to eliminate the acid (goodbye, heartburn; hello, flavor country).

---

Coffee isn't the only thing brewing at KnuckleBones. Innovative (think smoking) cocktails and a nightlife scene are part of the experiment.

*Lounge seating and an elegant bar setup are perfect for a social coffee or a work meeting.*

While he didn't study at the feet of Italian coffee connoisseurs, the KnuckleBones owner, who is from an area north of Mobile, did spend time in Chicago, where he learned about the finer art of libation preparation. He brought his skills back to Mobile and into KnuckleBones Elixir Co., where patience is its own reward—the coffee is extremely on point as are the trims and cuts at Beard and Blade. The Social Experiment is where you go if you care about your brew as much as your do.

## THE SOCIAL EXPERIMENT

**What:** Classic barbershop and experimental coffee and drinks lounge

**Where:** 202 Government St.

**Cost:** $3.50–$6 KnuckleBones; $20–$75 facial hair services

**Pro Tip:** Try a caramel Ferrero Rocher brownie at KnuckleBones with your coffee, and spring for the hot towel treatment at Beard and Blade.

# FOLLOW THE OYSTER TRAIL

## Where can I find oysters every way?

Once upon a time, wild oyster beds proliferated throughout Mobile Bay. Many who lived and worked on the bay off Dauphin Island Parkway's Cedar Point and Bayou La Batre remember painstakingly shucking oyster after oyster. Rampant oystering, though, depleted the beds, which take time to regrow. We learned too late that dredging was destroying oyster beds in such a way that they couldn't repopulate.

Oysters grow by affixing to the basin of the water. When they're dredged, what's left is soft muck. When efforts were made to regrow reefs, the new baby oysters sank into the sand and suffocated. There are now efforts being made to replenish this vital ecosystem as wild oyster reefs are essential for protecting shorelines, among other things. These are just some of the things you'll learn if you follow the Alabama Oyster Trail.

There are 25 stops on the full oyster trail, with 12 in downtown Mobile. The Oyster Trail stops are part of an interactive scavenger hunt that reveals how oysters affect our ecosystem and economy. You can recognize Oyster Trail stops because they're giant, beautifully painted oyster shell replicas positioned in relatively obvious points throughout downtown and along the coast.

---

Oyster City Brewing Company (OCBC) on Government Street isn't a Mobile staple; the brewery actually hails from Apalachicola, Florida, which is where most of the country's oysters are from.

*The 11th stop on the Oyster Trail was made by artist Devlin Wilson and features Wintzell's oyster-shucking legend Willie Brown hard at work.*

You'll also learn that most oyster harvests coming from Mobile Bay, Bayou La Batre, Dauphin Island, and surrounding waters are farmed oysters. Oyster farming is a helpful practice because it not only allows wild oyster reefs the opportunity to replant but it also creates a unique market for each of the farmers.

Boutique oysters that are exceptional in terms of size, presentation, and flavor are being cultivated at oyster farms and being devoured coastally as well as being shipped around the country. These large, plump oysters are the kind you eat raw, straight off the half shell.

## WINTZELL'S OYSTER HOUSE

**What:** Iconic coastal seafood restaurant where oysters are "fried, stewed, or nude"

**Where:** 605 Dauphin St. (plus other locations)

**Cost:** Market price; $12.99 half dozen / $21.99 dozen oysters

**Pro Tip:** Don't miss checking out a piece of the USS *Tecumseh* salvaged at Wintzell's flagship Dauphin Street restaurant.

# WEST INDIES SALAD

## Where can I find the original West Indies Salad (with a side of crab claws)?

Being the Port City, Mobile is known for fresh Gulf seafood. There's shrimp, crawfish, crab, oysters, flounder, catfish, and more in ready abundance. It should come as no surprise that two of the most iconic seafood dishes on menus around the world hailed from Mobile.

Once upon a time, Texan and former US Merchant Marine William "Bill" Bayley had settled in Mobile when he met Ethel, the Alabamian who'd become his wife. During his tenure, he served as a steward and stocked groceries for Alcoa Ship Lines. During a stop in the West Indies, Bayley made a quick-and-dirty meal of boiled lobster dressed up with a little olive oil, onions, and vinegar.

In 1947, Bayley's opened, and West Indies salad, prepared with fresh crabmeat instead of boiled lobster, graced the menu as an appetizer. It was a huge hit, as were the fried crab claws Bayley invented. Bayley initially tried boiled crab legs in butter but realized he had hit paydirt when he fried them (indeed, there's not a seafood restaurant in Mobile where you won't find fried crab claws).

They were the perfect appetizer. The restaurant grew to accommodate as many as 500 people during its heyday. When it closed during the 1970s, Bill's son and his late wife, Juanita, opened a smaller venue near the original, which is now a

Everything at Felix's is made with fresh, local seafood. Felix's is a few short minutes from the Battleship, which makes it the perfect place to fuel up before or refuel after a tour of the Mighty A!

*West Indies salad is a simple but elegant dish that has achieved icon-level status. It's one where the quality of your ingredients and the freshness of your seafood make all the difference.*

Greer's grocery store on Dauphin Island Parkway. The new venue was meant to be carryout only, but it quickly became a dine-in venue.

Many restaurants around town make West Indies Salad to perfection (it's key to chill and marinate the crabmeat for at least 24 hours) and there are many riffs on this classic as well as impeccable variations of crab claws to be found, arguably the best to be had is worth cruising for the causeway for their take on this icon at Felix's Fish Camp.

## FELIX'S FISH CAMP

**What:** Local seafood restaurant overlooking Mobile Bay

**Where:** 1530 Battleship Pkwy., Spanish Fort

**Cost:** $11–$25

**Pro Tip:** Sit by the window for beautiful bay views and end your evening with a sweet taste of Mobile—the Moon Pie A La Mode!

# JUBILEE BY THE SEA

## What's so special about a jubilee?

A jubilee is an event of great prosperity (biblically, the term means "prosperity"), and those around Mobile Bay know that the seafood jubilees that occur here are indeed prosperous. Some of the most desirable bay-dwelling seafood (crab, shrimp, flounder, catfish, eels, stingrays, etc.) washes to shore, stunned and ripe for the taking. People answer the jubilee bell by racing to the waterfront to collect as much as they can before the tide carries the spoils back to sea.

Jubilees have historically only occurred in two parts of the world: Mobile Bay and Tokyo Bay. The event is caused by a specific set of weather conditions that deoxygenate the water causing marine life to migrate increasingly closer to shore. While the uninformed call jubilees red tides and algae blooms and dismiss the phenomenon, it's actually simple science and is probably the only way some of us could catch a fish.

For a jubilee to occur, it needs to be windless, and water and air temperatures need to be warm. These conditions deplete the water's oxygen. The depletion leads to stratification with saline-rich water settling to the bottom of the bay and fresh water rising to the top.

When a breeze strong enough to move the topmost water layer blows, it causes hypoxic or deoxygenated water to rise and, with it, the fish. When the water is pushed shore bound, marine life rise and ride with the tide to shore.

## STEADMAN'S LANDING

**What:** Site of the 2020 jubilee on Mobile Bay

**Where:** Sibley St., Fairhope

**Cost:** Free

**Pro Tip:** The Steadman's Landing boardwalk is the perfect place for a sunset picnic overlooking Mobile Bay.

*Steadman's Landing, like the Middle Bay Lighthouse, suffered damage after the 1916 hurricane. Today's landing is a quiet respite with a flight of stairs leading to a secluded beach.*

Jubilees usually only happen between midnight and dawn because that's when oceanic oxygenation is lowest. The bounty is brief, hence the alarm bell. Marine life not harvested swim away when washed back into the bay.

The last jubilee occurred near Steadman's Landing in Montrose on Labor Day in 2020. Many live here their entire lives without seeing a jubilee. Nonetheless, seafood coveted during the jubilee can be found at the seafood restaurants throughout the Mobile Bay area.

Jubilees have been reported on the west side of Mobile Bay, which could reflect undesirable environmental changes, according to Ben Raines in *Saving America's Amazon.*

# AMERICA'S AMAZON

### Where can you see a 500-year-old cypress tree?

Veiny networks of rivers and waterways drain into the Mobile River system, which is an integral component of "America's Amazon," one of the planet's most productive and exotic ecosystems. Really. By the numbers, the Mobile–Tensaw River Delta hosts over a third of the freshwater fish species in North America; it's got more turtle species than any other river delta on earth, and it's the estuary where most of America's seafood is born.

While much is preserved, much has changed, and much is endangered. Cypress trees as large as California redwoods were once prolific in the delta; however, 150 years ago, these behemoths were logged for ship wood. Today, only one tree remains as a testament to the wonders of yesteryear.

The "Lord of the Delta," an ancient 500-year-old hollow cypress with a 27-foot circumference, can be found in Jessamine Bayou. It's a must-see for any adventurer. The journey to the tree is like something out of Tolkien. You arrive by boat and then trudge through a forest of knee-deep muddy water. The water level has to be just right to even attempt the trek to the tree.

Equally magical is that within the past 15 years, manatees have been spotted with increasing frequency by Mobilians. It was originally thought those spotted were lost, having wandered over from Florida (silly sea cows!); however, tracking

---

In 2004, Hurricane Ivan unearthed a 60,000-year-old cypress forest located 15 miles off the Mobile–Tensaw Delta. Research on the ancient forest reveals that the shoreline was once 30–60 miles farther out.

It's believed the Lord of the Delta was spared from being logged because it's hollow, and the wood wasn't worth the effort of cutting the tree down. The top of the tree is missing, possibly due to a lightning strike.

reveals that manatees habitually migrate between Mobile's waterways and Florida. They spend the warm season here and return to Florida when temperatures cool during our brief winter.

Manatees are easy to spot; they're between 9–10 feet long and usually hang out near the water's surface. While it's unlawful to touch manatees, spotting one bobbing along next to your paddleboard is nothing shy of amazing. The mouth of America's Amazon is indeed a wild world of wonder.

## AMERICA'S AMAZON ADVENTURES

**What:** A fun, safe, guided way to learn more about America's Amazon

**Where:** Charter tour location start points vary www.americasamazonadventures.com

**Cost:** $900 per tour (up to six per tour) or $150 per person

**Pro Tip:** Tours fill up fast; book early! The tour to the champion cypress includes a visit to the ancient Indian mounds.

# BLESSING OF THE FLEET

## What makes Alabama's "Seafood Capital" so prolific?

Bayou La Batre . . . it's not a work of fiction for Winston Groom's *Forrest Gump*; it's actually a place. Bayou La Batre is the small, mossy, Spanish oak–flanked fishing community southwest of Mon Louis Island and Highway 193, which leads to Dauphin Island.

First inhabited by the Mississippi Period Native Americans, Bayou La Batre was overtaken by Pierre Le Moyne d'Iberville and later by the Spanish. Bayou La Batre has a rich, multicultural history with French, Spanish, Portuguese, Greek, Mexican, and African influences, and the families who live in the bayou are families who've been here for generations.

These families have learned traditions, and one is showing gratitude for the abundance of fresh seafood harvested in Bayou La Batre, also known as Alabama's Seafood Capital, in a tradition known as the Blessing of the Fleet. The tradition is hundreds of years old and is practiced around the world.

On the first Sunday of May, a special Mass is held to bless the fishermen and their vessels to ensure good fishing. Clarence Mallet revived the time-honored European tradition in Bayou La Batre, and the first blessing took place in 1949, and it was a

---

### ST. MARGARET'S CATHOLIC CHURCH

**What:** The church where the annual Blessing of the Fleet transpires

**Where:** 13790 S Wintzell Ave., Bayou La Batre

**Cost:** Free

**Pro Tip:** The Mass is Sunday at 10 a.m.; the land parade is at 2 p.m.; and the boat parade is at 3. If you miss it . . . bless your heart.

The Papa Rod *shrimp boat is moored in the bayou during the blessing festival.*

humble affair where bread, lettuce, tomato, and boiled shrimp were served (what we call a po' boy; though, then the shrimp is often fried).

Today's event is a weekend affair with a gumbo cook-off the Saturday prior, a juried decorated boat parade, an arts and crafts show, boat cruises, and bingo. The following morning, the sacred blessing takes place and is followed by the land parade and then the boat parade.

It's a spectacular sight and is a unique way to actively participate in history in the making.

---

Scalawags and pirates hid illicit bounties in Portersville Bay. When the nightly fog rolls in, the spirits of the departed are discernible by a chill breeze and the scent of rum.

# PRETTY FLY PLACE

## What's one of the most popular birding spots in the country?

Many are surprised to learn that coastal Mobile, Dauphin Island in particular, is among the most popular areas in the country for bird watching. In the fall and spring, migratory birds leave and return to the US. Their last stop before setting sail across the Gulf of Mexico is Dauphin Island, making it a wildly popular spot to see rare and exotic bird species.

Dauphin Island is home to 11 protected birding sanctuaries and swamps, and the Dauphin Island Birding Checklist identifies 367 of the 446 species of bird found in Alabama. The Alabama Birding Trails websites delves into even more detail specifying areas around the Gulf Coast where birds can be spotted. This includes the Mobile–Tensaw Delta Five Rivers area and Gaillard Island.

Gaillard Island is a unique man-made plot created by the US Army Corps of Engineers. It's the result of requisite dredging in Mobile Bay. The island is a nesting ground for the once heavily

**DAUPHIN ISLAND BIRD SANCTUARIES**

**What:** The best birding spots on Dauphin Island

**Where:** coastalbirding.org for a checklist and map

**Cost:** Free

**Pro Tip:** The best birding moments happen early in the day, so get a good night's sleep and rise with the sun (or before).

The wooded stroll at the Dauphin Island Cadillac Square sanctuary ends on a remote strip beach where you can sit and take photos of birds landing on the sand.

*Author, artist, and photographer Susan Rouillier made capturing images of birds like these great egrets her life's work a decade ago. Top left and right photo courtesy of Susan Rouillier*

endangered brown pelicans. People can visit the island located 20 minutes from shore, but they aren't allowed to set foot there or to disturb the nesting pelicans.

In fact, look but don't touch is the general rule of thumb when it comes to identifying and admiring the birds that reside and that pass through this area (not that many birds would allow it). Instead, bring binoculars, sunblock, and a camera along with your checklist and make a game of testing your budding birding skills.

# WE ARE THE RAINIEST?

## How does sunny Mobile get the most rain in the US?

In many places, conversations about the weather mean that people are *bored*. Not so in Mobile. The weather is a topic of conversation that we discuss with rapt attention. Our meteorologists are regarded with the same level of reverence as the papacy (or close enough). Everything is planned around weather, which has the temperament of a toddler that missed its nap.

Mobile can experience all four seasons in a week . . . sometimes, in a day. There have been many days that have started out 80 degrees and sunny, experienced a brief apocalypse midday, and concluded freezing (in the 60s) and hailing. We have fun.

Loads of laundry reveal weeks that have necessitated jeans, long underwear, and down jackets as well as swimwear and tank tops. On average, Mobile is seasonally warm, and our winters are brief (November to maybe February and a week or so in March). The capricious temperatures usually come during periods of transition, which I suppose could be called spring and fall.

Spring is a wonderful time (unless you have allergies, in which case, try not to breathe), barring the weekly monsoon. The weather will be gorgeous in the 70s for days and then ominous doom where the rain falls in sheets and you fall into a delirious sleep to the soothing intonation of tornado warnings on your phone.

*Carpe Diem on Old Shell Road offers a cozy cottage environment perfect for weathering any rainstorm.*

Still, we love spring because too soon it's summer. Temperatures somehow vault from the 70s to the 90s between April and May—like they're trying to sneak in—and stay that way throughout the summer, when Mobile sits roughly three feet from the sun until October. On the plus side, a daily summer rain cools things off. Between these deluges and the spring monsoons and hurricanes, Mobile gets more rain than any other city in the US.

Mobile gets 67 inches of rain per year. Dodge the downpour at a local coffee shop where you can weather watch. Showers are typically heavy but short.

# SEE YOU LATER, ALLIGATOR!

## Where can I (safely) see alligators?

People get oddly wary when you talk about kayaking or paddleboarding around the delta and adjacent rivers. Yes, alligators do inhabit these waters, but they're not likely to bother you (they aren't crocodiles, to which you look delicious). Alligators are actually pretty chill in that they like to loll around on the sides of the river and keep to themselves. Unless you start throwing raw beef tips into the water, they're not going to approach you.

This is why airboat rides are so fun and are such a "best-kept secret" of Mobile . . . even though we have a lot of water surrounding us and are literally considered the mouth of America's Amazon, people associate airboat rides to view alligators sunbathing in their natural habitats with places like Louisiana and Florida, but they live here, too.

Fully grown, alligators can be 12 feet and can live up to 50 years. Many of the alligators spotted here are young. Baby alligators are easy to distinguish because of their smaller size. Of course, these are things you'll learn on the tour. You'll also learn that due to unregulated hunting, alligators were once endangered back in 1967. In 1987, they were elevated to just being threatened, and that's largely due to habitat loss caused by environmental changes.

---

Look for brown pelicans; they're the reason the US National Wildlife Refuge System was created. Hunted in the 1900s, these coastal dwellers were almost wiped out again by biocides.

*Airboats are great for fishing and exploring, since they don't have rudders and can glide at rapid speeds across the top of the water. Photos courtesy of Airboat Adventures*

Alligators aren't the only wildlife indigenous to this area you'll encounter on an airboat ride through the delta. Pelicans, herons, hawks, owls, eagles, osprey, and falcons are frequently spotted. Turtles and multiple fish species abound as well. You'll see cypress trees, seagrass, and river flora as well. It's a safe way to experience nature and a way few have taken advantage of to see a threatened species.

## AIRBOAT ADVENTURES

**What:** A guided tour through the Mobile–Tensaw Delta

**Where:** 3775 Battleship Pkwy. (next to Bluegill)

**Cost:** $40–$50 per person, depending on the type of tour

**Pro Tip:** Airboat Adventures only tours from February 1 to November 14.

# ESTUARIUM DEEP DIVE

## Does Alabama have an aquarium?

When most people think of aquariums, they think of massive facilities full of marine life from all over the planet, a mascot or two, and some kind of show—dolphins, sea lions, etc. With this expectation, it's not a surprise that most people don't think of the Dauphin Island Sea Lab (DISL) as Alabama's aquarium, but it is (and, frankly, it's a lot cooler than touristy aquariums).

Dauphin Island Sea Lab opened in the early '70s as a marine sciences research facility; it wouldn't be until the '90s that the estuarium (now the Alabama Aquarium) was open to the public. Because Mobile is home to the fourth-largest estuary in the US, the focus of the sea lab is on what happens in our local estuary. Specifically, areas of focus are Mobile Bay, the Mobile–Tensaw Delta, the Gulf of Mexico, and the Barrier Islands.

The exhibit has a 7,000-gallon stingray touch pool and 31 aquariums with over 100 species of plant and marine life

### ALABAMA AQUARIUM

**What:** Research aquarium focused on Mobile's aquatic ecosystem

**Where:** 102 Bienville Blvd., Dauphin Island

**Cost:** $12 adult, $6 children 5–18, $10 seniors 60+

**Pro Tip:** Visit during one of the twice-monthly free boardwalk talks to get even more out of the experience.

DISL operates a free real-time coastal observing system called ARCOS that tracks wind, precipitation, salinity, and more. Hurricane Sally damaged some of the stations.

*The boardwalk is a unique interactive feature of the Alabama Aquarium. Photos courtesy of Alabama Aquarium*

on display. The coolest part, though, may be the Living Marsh Boardwalk, which allows visitors to interact with nature.

Local marine researchers offer many lectures through the Alabama Aquarium that explain local phenomenon, such as the migratory habits of manatees. The aquarium also offers adventurous family camps—including one that lets you kayak through a salt marsh and go on a crab hunt. It's definitely one of our best-kept secrets.

# DOGGIE PADDLE

## Where's the best place to kick back in a kayak?

Mobile's home to a unique aquatic ecosystem and its eponymous bay is the fourth-largest drainage basin in North America. A network of braided rivers flow through Alabama and into the Mobile Bay Watershed. In short: there's a lot of water and plenty of places to kayak, but if you're looking to have a relaxed kayaking adventure and a chat with locals, Dog River on a Monday evening is where you need to be.

The Kayak with Keve paddling group formed on Facebook in June 2015. The story so goes that founding member, Keve, met a woman who lived off Dauphin Island Parkway during Art Walk in downtown Mobile. When Keve found out the woman had a river in her backyard, he asked if he could launch a kayak from her home. Of course, she agreed . . . and asked if she could join. A small, friendly agreement quickly ballooned into a Monday night ritual shared among a motley crew of friendly, happy people who know it's the little things in life that make the whole thing worth living.

### DOG RIVER PARK

**What:** A public boat launch into Dog River

**Where:** 2459 Dog River Dr. N

**Cost:** Free

**Noteworthy:** The Wallace Pier, where the Kayak with Keve paddle starts, is visible from this public launch point.

Dog River was allegedly named so in 1702 by d'Iberville because an alligator purportedly ate one of his companion's dogs when they camped there on their trek to 27-Mile Bluff.

*Kayakers appreciate Dog River's natural splendor; though, it's also an archeological landmine. One excavation by University of South Alabama researchers revealed 170,000 findings from colonial and antebellum periods.*

Paddles start at 5:30 and last a couple hours. The group starts at the Wallace Pier (you can launch at the Navco Road Boat Launch and paddle over to meet the group), and you make your way to a marshy area of cordgrass and bulrush affectionately called "the Dog Bone," where the kayakers settle in, pop open their beverage of choice, and kick back to watch the sun set over the evergreens. Kayak with Keve devotees are the only people in Mobile whose favorite night of the week is Monday. Joining a Monday-night paddle is the perfect way for the kayak curious to get on the water and make new friends.

# HIP, HIP HIPPIE BEACH

## Where do the river rats hang out?

Summers in Mobile start around mid-May and last through September. During leisure time, the average Mobilian can be found on the water in a boat or a kayak or just dipping their toes in. Many of these folks identify as "river rats," which are laid-back summer lovers who just want to have a good time.

**HIPPIE BEACH**

**What:** Secret beach off Halls Mill Creek

**Where:** 30.6041 degrees N, 88.1407 degrees W

**Cost:** Free

**Pro Tip:** Bring sunblock, a bag for your trash, a picnic, and something to sit on. Oh, and watch out for alligators.

With Dauphin Island being a solid 45-minute drive from the city, many look for more accessible places to hang out on a random sunny afternoon. For those who know, Hippie Beach on Halls Mill Creek off Dog River is the place to be. It's the perfect place to do . . . "hippie things."

By hippie things, we mean eat cold fried chicken (seriously), drink something cold and frosty, soak up the sun, and generally do nothing. Kids play with whatever toys they brought with them or they dig around in the sand while the adults lounge on chairs or wade knee-deep into the water to stay semi-cool while they chat. It's the pinnacle of simple living.

Hippie Beach is private property, but it's accessible to the public so long as everyone behaves responsibly and cleans up after themselves. Littering is a major no-no at Hippie Beach.

*Even though it's a stone's throw from Halls Mill Creek Landing, you'll feel like you're in the middle of nowhere when hanging at Hippie Beach.*

Just past Hippie Beach, just around the bend, you'll eventually come to two fun and interesting destinations. One is a slide mounted in a tree. This is a lot more common than you think on the river. Many a river rat affixes a sliding board to a tree with a ladder for when the tide is high enough to use it. There's also a tire on a rope swing, which makes for lots of kid-friendly fun. Again, the tide has to be at the right height to climb off it and swing into the cool, shaded water. Obviously, you have to use your judgment on the water depth. Regardless, it's a beautiful detour to take when spending the day lazing at Hippie Beach.

# SUP, Y'ALL?

## Where can I learn to stand-up paddleboard?

With so much water surrounding Mobile, you'd be remiss not to spend some of your time on it. You've probably seen stand-up paddleboarding (SUP). Those are the people who seemingly float on the top of water on a long, narrow board balancing with what must be impeccable skills that took the better part of their childhood to master. And then there are the people out there doing yoga (as if your chakras could take that kind of pressure).

While SUPing looks hard, the secret truth is that it's actually very easy. Boards are wide enough that you're able to maintain your balance in almost any aquatic condition. Boards are also specially designed for specific tasks like general touring, yoga, racing, river, surf, and wind sailing.

If you've ever wanted to give SUPing a try, you can on Dauphin Island. Pure Aloha Adventures offers paddleboard rentals as well as lessons, so if you already know what you're doing, just rent a board and hit the water.

The lessons are appropriate for kids ages six and up. It's recommended that rentals and lessons be booked in the

**PURE ALOHA ADVENTURES**

**What:** Aloe Bay, where you meet for SUP lessons on Dauphin Island

**Where:** 1102 De Soto Ave., Dauphin Island

**Cost:** $49 kids 6–10; $59 ages 11+

**Pro Tip:** Bring backup clothes and/or wear a swimsuit. Even if you don't fall in, you might get wet.

SUPing is a great way to get exercise because you work all your muscle groups to propel the board.

*The world feels like a peaceful place when you're on a SUP. Photos courtesy of Bucky Hicks*

morning when winds are at their lowest. Unless you like to feel like a plastic bag in a hurricane, you'll want placid waters for your first SUPing experience.

It takes only a few minutes to orient to the sensation of standing on the board on the water. The board is surprisingly stable. By the end, you'll think, "That was easy . . . what was I so worried about?"

Dauphin Island's Aloe Bay is the perfect spot to get your feet wet on a SUP. Most people have the will, but they don't know there's a way. Now that you know, say "aloha" to new experiences.

# GAME, SET, MATCH

## Where can I find one of the world's largest public tennis facilities?

While football reigns supreme throughout the South in general, tennis is the sport of choice in Mobile. Many may be surprised to learn that the Mobile Tennis Center in Langan Park is one of the world's largest public tennis facilities—and has been so for years.

The Mobile Tennis Center at Langan Park has 60 lit (lit as in lighted, but they are also cool) Laykold hard courts. A well-stocked pro shop and stringers mean total tennis all the time. That's not an exaggeration. There are times when a player can't get a court because they're all booked.

The Mobile Tennis Center was built at Municipal Park in 1958. Back then, it had only eight courts. A handful of notorious local families were instrumental in its foundation. In a few decades, it grew and became the go-to for major tennis tournaments, including the NCCAA, AHSAA, and NAIA tournaments.

---

**MOBILE TENNIS CENTER**

**What:** One of the world's largest public tennis centers

**Where:** 851 Gaillard Dr.

**Cost:** $2–$5, depending on age and time of match

**Pro Tip:** Call ahead and register for a clinic. You can never work too hard on that backhand!

---

Mobile Tennis Center is located at Langan Park, home to Azalea City Golf Course, the Mobile Botanical Gardens, and the Mobile Museum of Art.

*The Mobile Tennis Center, captured from above, draws tennis afficionados from around the country.*

Most prominent is the Serve It Up with Love tournament, Alabama's largest tennis tournament. The event transpires over several days and involves participation from upwards of 500 players. Proceeds go to support the Child Advocacy Center. It's literally an event based on love played by a game that starts with a score of love and is played out of love regardless of the score. Now . . . who's serving?

# VAULTING ABOUT TOWN

## Why do people pole-vault through downtown?

Sometimes, it's best not to ask questions . . . and asking *how* or *why* there's a Dauphin Street Vault is one of those instances (but I'll tell you anyway). Once a year, the third Saturday of July, Dauphin Street Vault lines the entertainment district's downtown streets and allows entrants of all ages and skill levels to compete. Olympians, professionals, and your neighbor (you're pretty sure his name is Justin) who peaked in high school (if he peaked at all) can, have, and will compete. Seriously, though, a lot of serious athletes from all over the country attend this unique event.

Now in its 11th year, the Dauphin Street Pole Vault is achieving new heights (pun intended). For the athletes, many of whom come from out of town for a weekend of frivolity, it's a chance to compete. For the locals, it's a chance to sit back, have a few drinks, eat some kind of painfully un-athletic dish (like a bacon burger with an egg and a fried onion on it because we're not jumping), and cheer on the real heroes.

---

**DAUPHIN STREET VAULT**

**What:** Pole-vaulting competition every third Saturday of July in Mobile

**Where:** Approximately 256 Dauphin St.

**Cost:** Free

**Pro Tip:** BYO chair, sunblock, and some bottled water. It's a hot day spent outdoors, but you won't want to miss a minute of it.

---

Pole-vaulting dates back to ancient Greece, though it didn't become an Olympic event until the Sydney games in 2000. US athlete Stacy Dragila took home the first gold.

*Athletes sail above watching crowds at the Dauphin Street Vault.*
*Photo courtesy of Ann Esposito and Mobile Sports Authority*

The pole vault is a nonprofit grassroots event to raise awareness about pole-vaulting. Over 250 athletes enter the competition. It's very impressive, and speaking for the spectators, the thing we often leave most aware of (other than that we probably ate too much . . . it happens) is how remarkably unathletic we are in comparison to pole-vaulters. It's good to stay humble.

# URBAN WILDERNESS

## Where's a great nature hike around Mobile?

Coastal and largely flat, Mobile is not the place you think of for mountain biking and wilderness hiking and trail running (Cheryl Strayed's book *Wild* would've been a lot shorter if she'd have tried to hike here). It's true, you really can't have it all, but even though Mobile doesn't have a mountain range spilling through it, we do still have nature trails.

Some of the best—and best-kept secrets—are located on the University of South Alabama campus. For hikers and trail runners, there's the Glenn Sebastian Nature Trail. Professor Emeritus Glenn Sebastian was one of the most beloved geography teachers at the university. His career spanned 40 years (1967–2007), and he touched many students with his passion and his wit. Sebastian's jokes could liven up any 8 a.m. lecture. He took his students on many trips in and around and out of the US to better understand nature.

Opened after the professor and former park ranger retired, the Glenn Sebastian Nature Trail boasts 95 acres of wooded hiking area. There are five different path options: a 1-mile loop, a 1.5-mile loop, a 2-mile loop, a 2.5-mile loop, and a 5K loop. Trails are marked by colored signs.

The trails are pet friendly, but domesticated animals must be on leashes, and their droppings should not be left behind.

## GLENN SEBASTIAN TRAIL

**What:** Hiking and trail jogging loop series named for esteemed professor

**Where:** Aubrey Green Dr.

**Cost:** Free

**Pro Tip:** Bring bug spray and a camera; watch out for snakes—poisonous copperhead snakes blend right in with the leaves.

*The Glenn Sebastian Trail is abutted by a lake and features several signs with inspirational quotes on the trail.*

While cyclists are more than welcome to use this trail, the nearby South Alabama mountain bike trails off John Counts Drive near the new Hancock Whitney Stadium are even better; the beginner loop is a 3.5-mile trail; the intermediate loop is an 8-mile trail; the advanced loop is a 12.4-mile trail.

The only criteria for riding are BYOB (bring your own bike), watch for wildlife, and trails are only open dusk to dawn. Safety first.

Walk onto the footbridge next to the nature trail. Cranes, turtles, and more have been spotted here. Abide the signs, though, and watch out for alligators.

# SECRET GARDEN CITY

## Where are the secret gardens of Mobile?

Mobile has lots of quirky secrets, but there are a lot of beautiful secrets, too—they're just easy to miss if you're not paying attention. Take the secret gardens. Mobile has many little garden spaces accessible to the public tucked in and around the city.

Two spaces in particular are worth the quest. The first is a meditative one-acre retreat tucked off Government Street. Called the Cornerstone Gardens, the space serves as a secluded spot in nature for centering, connecting, and finding balance.

The owner, Vaughn Drinkard, said people would wander up to the gate, so after a while he started opening the gate indicating that the gardens are open and that visitors are welcome. The elusive Cornerstone Gardens space is a blissful respite from the world, and it's surprisingly easy to miss on busy Government Street.

Equally beautiful, remote, and off the beaten path is the Japanese garden at the Mobile Botanical Gardens. Like Cornerstone Gardens, the Japanese garden was founded by a passionate visionary. In this case, it was Charles Woods who manifested the Japanese garden, which now exists to teach visitors about the culture of Japan.

A large koi pond as well as plant life indigenous to Japan, such as the Alabama state flower (the camellia), Japanese magnolias, lotus blossoms, cherry blossoms, and more proliferate in the garden.

---

### JAPANESE GARDEN

**What:** 14-acre Japanese style garden

**Where:** 700 Forest Hill Dr.

**Cost:** Free, but donations are accepted

**Pro Tip:** Every first and third Tuesday morning, the Japanese Studies Center located at the garden hosts a Sumi-e Japanese Art Class.

*You can make an appointment for a paid visit to the Cornerstone Gardens at 1066 Government by calling 251-298-7670.*

On the remainder of the botanical gardens site, you'll find nature trails that sprawl three miles and that lead to Three-Mile Creek. There are six trails in all, and they delve deep into the woods, giving you a unique up-close-and-personal look at residential wildlife.

It's the perfect place to get off the beaten path. You forget you're in the heart of a bustling metropolis by ducking into these peaceful local parks that are hidden in plain sight.

A small garden space surrounds the Cathedral of the Immaculate Conception on Government. It's accessible from the side of the portico and surrounds the cathedral.

# PIRATE'S POOL

### Where can I let out my inner carouser with my hearties?

In the summer, the heat index and humidity will melt your face. It's hotter than Mordor (probably) because at least that was a dry heat. When the temperatures get hot, there's nothing more refreshing than kicking it at the pool with a bushwhacker. Bonus points if there's also a beach nearby.

Down on Dauphin Island off the main road in a "if you know, you know" kind of place, you'll find an old-Florida 1950s-style circular diner called Pirate's Bar and Grill. You don't have to be a pirate to go, but you do have to pay to park and to hang out at the pool.

The circular saltwater pool is flanked by picnic tables, lounge chairs, and palm trees. There's an outdoor bar, so you don't have to go into the restaurant, which has amazing panoramic views of the Gulf of Mexico, to order food and drinks. (And by "drinks," we mean bushwhackers, because that's Pirate's signature drink, even though the sweet, frozen rum-based concoction was created on St. Thomas in 1975. It makes sense that it was created on an island, since it's now a staple of island-style bars and eateries.)

People who hang out at Pirate's know to plan to spend the day at the historic haunt. Past the bar, you can slide onto the sand and walk down to the water and watch seagulls and pelicans fly overhead. Sailboats and parasailers dot the horizon,

Wednesdays are the deliciously popular Wing Night at Pirate's. During the spring and summer, local artists play live music on Wednesdays from about 5–9.

*With its unique circular structure, Pirate's Bar and Grill is a retro getaway at the Isle Dauphine Golf Club.*

and it's easy to forget that you haven't absconded to some distant land or landed in someone else's life. Suffice to say, if this is how pirates chill when the sun is blazing . . . we could all get used to it.

## PIRATE'S BAR AND GRILL

**What:** Historic retro publicly accessible pool and beach

**Where:** 100 Orleans Dr., Dauphin Island

**Cost:** $9.50 for a bushwhacker, pool access $6, beach access $5, combo access $10

**Pro Tip:** You must wear shoes and a shirt or dress to enter the restaurant.

# THE CRICHTON LEPRECHAUN

## Where da gold at?

St. Patrick's Day is largely celebrated on March 17 each year. The day in most US cities is characterized as a good debauch starting in the morning and lasting into the wee hours of the evening. Irish music, corned beef, green beer, and good times are had by all. Mobile, having a reasonably high population of Irish immigrants (or just Irish-blended citizens), has historically found a way to enjoy the spirited day at a smattering of Irish venues throughout the city.

That all changed in 2006. In 2006, NBC news affiliate WPMI-TV broke the now-and-forever-viral news story about the Crichton Leprechaun. The now-legendary Crichton Leprechaun was allegedly sighted in a tree. Thankfully, thanks to an amateur sketch, which was shown in all seriousness during the newscast, we have a rough idea of what the leprechaun seen in Crichton looks like.

### CALLAGHAN'S IRISH SOCIAL CLUB

**What:** An Irish pub with the best burgers in town

**Where:** 916 Charleston St.

**Cost:** Free to hang out on St. Patrick's Day; menu prices for drinks and food

**Pro Tip:** Callaghan's has a killer Sunday brunch and the best Bloody Mary in town.

Importantly, the leprechaun, which could be a shadow cast by a tree branch, allegedly vanishes if a light is shined in his direction. One Mobilian asserts that the leprechaun is a "crackhead" that got ahold of the wrong stuff and thought it'd be a good idea to get into the tree to impersonate the leprechaun. Frankly, that theory fits, but don't tell the children.

*To ring in the day, many locals head to Callaghan's Irish Social Club, a frequent "best burger" winner once co-owned by New Orleans Saint Chuck Commiskey.*

Another citizen said he has a magical leprechaun flute that had been in his family for hundreds of years, while another indicated that he wanted to dig the tree up with a backhoe because he wants to "know where da gold at." With inflation, so do the rest of us.

The video and the Crichton Leprechaun have become cult classics in Mobile with koozies, T-shirts, window stickers, and more available in honor of our locally legendary St. Patrick's Day tradition.

Before it became one of Mobile's most beloved restaurants, the 1920s building Callaghan's is housed in was once a meat market.

# THAT'S JUST NUTS

## What's up with the squirrels in Bienville Square?

Bienville Square, located at 150 Dauphin St., started its life as a city park in 1824. The picturesque grassy square comprises sprawling live oaks, iron benches, commemorative plaques and memorials (one of which honors the longest-living *Clotilda* survivor in Mobile, Cudjoe Lewis), and an iron fountain installed in 1889–90. (The fountain replaced the cast iron deer that had previously occupied the central space. The deer now resides in Washington Square Park.)

While the park's aesthetic, wrought iron works, and converging sidewalks are certainly a large part of its appeal, the real lure of Bienville Square is undoubtedly those nutty squirrels. The squirrels, which were allegedly brought into the square over a century ago to make the park more inviting have . . . well, they've taken over. Despite this, people can't get enough of these furry friends.

The Bienville squirrels have grown so accustomed to being fed peanuts from the nearby A & M Peanut Shop on Dauphin Street that they've proliferated and domesticated. House cats are more skittish than these squirrels.

Really. The Bienville squirrels do not flee when they see humans. Rather, they observe humans with contemplative curiosity and adopt expectant postures in anticipation of the savory morsel many offer.

---

A Joe Cain Marching Society People's Parade Group called the Mystic Squirrels of Bienville (Mystic SOBs) throws peanuts from A & M Peanut Shop during the parade.

*Bienville Square is just one of many stops on the popular Oyster Trail in downtown Mobile.*

With few predators and plenty of food, the squirrel situation became so overwhelming that Mayor Sandy Stimpson ordained they should not be fed, and in 2022, a deportation effort was implemented to thin the Bienville squirrel population.

While part of this effort had to do with population control, another had to do with preserving Bienville's trees. The oaks that flank Bienville Square give the landmark its characteristic charm. The trees are what make it so lovely to spend an afternoon strolling Bienville Square, eating treats from the A & M Peanut Shop, and making furry friends.

## A & M PEANUT SHOP

**What:** Nostalgic mainstay since 1947 for fresh-roasted peanuts and treats

**Where:** 209 Dauphin St.

**Cost:** Varies

**Pro Tip:** Experience downtown Mobile the old-fashioned way. Grab a hot dog from the Wacked Out Weiner next to A & M and take your picnic to Bienville Square.

# FILM, FORREST, FILM

## How can I see Mobile on the silver screen?

In 1994, *Forrest Gump*, a movie based on late Fairhope historian and author Winston Groom's novel of the same title, opened to meteoric box office success. The central story is about a mentally challenged Alabama man named Forrest Gump who seemingly stumbles through a variety of history's most significant events.

Forrest's mental handicap allows Groom to reveal history though an unfiltered lens in much the same way Mark Twain does in the *Adventures of Huckleberry Finn*. Through Forrest, we observe war, systemic oppression, racism, veterans' affairs, and more. We also watch the simple-yet-complex love story of a man who loves a woman who—because of her childhood trauma—does not learn to love herself until it's too late. It's all very poignant.

Many wonder if the film was shot in Alabama, and while we'd love to say yes, the answer is no. While there is most definitely a Bayou La Batre, located off the Mississippi Sound in Mobile County, Alabama lacked the financial incentives to justify a full movie being shot here.

*Forrest Gump* was filmed on the Atlantic Coast. The famous bus scene was shot in Savannah, while those allegedly in Bayou La Batre took place in Beaufort, South Carolina.

The Entertainment Industry Incentive Act of 2009 opened things up for Alabama, and several movies have since been shot

---

**MOBILE'S LAST ALLEYWAY**

**What:** Setting of car chase scene in Nicolas Cage film

**Where:** Beside 8 St. Joseph St.

**Cost:** Free

**Pro Tip:** Walk down the alley during the day; afterward, reward your curiosity with a pastry from Pollman's Bake Shop on the corner.

*Bayou La Batre is where Forrest Gump played by Tom Hanks earned his riches in the eponymous movie adapted from the book written by late Fairhope author Winston Groom.*

in Alabama. Prior to the incentive, the city's main claim to cinematic fame was Steven Spielberg's *Close Encounters of the Third Kind*. Brookley Field was used for the famed spaceship scene, as was the Bankhead Tunnel.

The Bankhead is still the most notable setting; though, Big Bayou Canot is often championed for its role in the bridge scene in *The Lost Boys* (1987). Likewise, the USS *Alabama* was a major setting for *Under Siege* (1992). *Back Roads* (1980) with Sally Field and Tommy Lee Jones was filmed in and around the Mobile area. Lastly, another major film credit prior to the 2009 film incentive bill, which garnered more cinematic activity in Mobile, was Al Pacino's *The Insider* (1999) where Mobile was a standing-in for New Orleans.

---

*Heist* (2015) with Robert DeNiro was filmed in the Crystal Ballroom of the Battle House Hotel. Nicolas Cage enjoyed time at the same hotel pool when not filming *Tokarev* (2013).

# SEE ART, WALK

## Where can I see what local artists are up to?

Mobile has a vibrant arts scene, as evidenced by the increasing number of murals painted on buildings and by the brilliant recycling of the storm-damaged Bienville live oaks implemented via the Mobile Arts Council. Art is all around us in Mobile; the city is a veritable panoply of innovation, ideation, and lunacy (you did read about Eugene Walter, right?). It's what makes it great . . . but . . . where do you see the genius at work?

The answer is the LoDa ArtWalks. Every second Friday from 6–9 p.m., Dauphin Street and neighboring streets spark to life with artists and artisans. Local galleries like the Center for the Living Arts and the Mobile Arts Council on Joachim Street, as well as other shops (ahem, Haunted Book Shop), open their doors for things like book signings, meet and greets with the artists, and shopping.

Musicians play in Cathedral Square, just as they do during the fall and winter Cathedral Square Market in the Park Saturdays when local farmers and artisans (think goat milk soap and Amish butter and homemade dog treats) sell their creations.

Many ArtWalks are themed; for example, in October, one of the float barn designers leads a parade of masked marauders donning giant Diá de los Muertos masks, and April nods to tie-dye and kites, and May celebrates photography for National

---

ArtWalks also celebrates the culinary arts; SOCU Southern Kitchen and Oyster Bar is owned by Mobile native chef Erica Barrett, who was featured on Food Network's *Raid the Fridge*.

*A mural painted by local artist Ginger Woechan overlooks Cathedral Square where the Festival of Flowers took place in spring 2022.*

Photography Month and pets because May is also National Pet Month. Speaking of pets, since the LoDa ArtWalks are largely outdoors, they're both pet and kid friendly. June's ArtWalk, naturally, will celebrate pride.

The LoDa ArtWalk Facebook page has additional information allowing local art lovers and the art curious to stay tuned and to stay in touch.

## LODA ARTWALK

**What:** Walking arts event in downtown Mobile

**Where:** 6 S Joachim St.

**Cost:** Free

**Pro Tip:** Park near the Garage and walk your way all the way down to Royal Street. Make dinner reservations in advance . . . you may not find anywhere to walk in during ArtWalk.

# FOLKS BOND AT THE POND

## Where can I go to hear great music and live like a local?

First, it's important to preface this by saying that when you're asking a Mobilian how to live like a local, you need to know if you're talking to a city mouse, a country mouse, or a hippie mouse. A city mouse will tell you the best places to eat in downtown and which cucumbers to request for your spa sesh at the Battle House. A country mouse will tell you where to get good bait on the way to Dauphin Island. And a hippie mouse will tell you about the outdoor folk concert, the Frog Pond Sunday Social.

Out at Blue Moon Farm in Silverhill, owner Cathe Steele, modeled the Frog Pond socials after the laid-back outdoor "Midnight Rambles" concerts conducted by gravel-throated Woodstock drummer Levon Helm. At Frog Pond, you'll find singers lined up on the rainbow fairy-lit "wood porch" under a 200-year-old cedar tree.

### FROG POND SUNDAY SOCIAL

**What:** Farm Folk Alliance house concerts by local legends

**Where:** 19375 Rada Rd., Silverhill

**Cost:** $30–$40 (all proceeds go to the songwriters)

**Pro Tip:** Check the Facebook page for event dates and times, and call 251-232-3072 for an invitation to attend a social.

The Frog Pond Sunday Social is a Folk Alliance event; the Folk Alliance International is a nonprofit dedicated to sustaining the folk genre and community worldwide.

*Blues-Americana singer-songwriter Grayson Capps performs at the Frog Pond Sunday Social to an appreciative audience. Photos courtesy of Chad Edwards/ MCE Photography*

If you're wondering how good the music is . . . Steele knows good music. Steele happens to have been the manager responsible for the epic musical lineup at the iconic Pirate's Cove haunt in Josephine, so the folksy tunes at the intimate social are beyond on point.

It's a BYO chair, drink, and a covered dish to share for the potluck, if you don't mind, along with an entry donation of $30 or $40. Out-of-towners are welcome to camp if they don't feel like driving back to wherever they came from (always a fun and rustic experience).

Because it's a little ways out of town and because you have to secure an invitation to attend, it's a lesser-known but truly amazing event held in the confines of wholesome nature among happy-go-lucky music lovers.

# CEDAR STREET SOCIAL CLUB

## Where are they making music and meals in Mobile?

Once a part of downtown Mobile's network of streetcar lines, Cedar Street grew desolate for a period of years. That changed in 2018 when native Mobilian and former MLB pitcher Jake Peavy returned to the Port City to shake things up.

Musician, philanthropist, innovator, and father Peavy invested with developer Matt LeMond in the area between Dauphin and St. Francis streets. Music was an outlet for Peavy during his years playing for the San Diego Padres, Chicago White Sox, Boston Red Sox, and San Francisco Giants, so it's no surprise music was how he reconnected with his hometown.

Peavy formed a team of friends and family and got to work. At the heart of things is Dauphin Street Sound, an inclusive recording studio committed to producing quality music and embracing the vibrant mixed-genre music culture. The studio has a legitimate hippie vibe that spills into the happenings at Cedar Street.

The Cedar Street Social Club is an established musical venue with shows, benefits, and motley picking sessions throughout the week. It really is all about the music at Cedar Street. A new outdoor seating area called the Outsider serves as a place where people can hang out and people watch, listen to music, sip drinks, and snack on local bites.

---

### CEDAR STREET SOCIAL CLUB

**What:** Popular bar and hip music venue

**Where:** 4 N Cedar St., #2106

**Cost:** $5+

**Pro Tip:** Stop by a on Tuesday night when local musicians gather to pick and play.

---

*Ivan Neville joins in on the piano at a Cedar Street show on Mardi Gras Day 2021.*

The Insider, meanwhile, is a collaboration in the making. LeMond, who loves Peavy's innovative spirit, is working with him to improve Mobile through innovation and philanthropy. The Insider is a restaurant incubator that allows restaurateurs to test and refine concepts before investing in bigger venues. Meanwhile, it will all just keep bringing people together.

In the future, Peavy hopes to bring another big music festival back to the rapidly revitalizing city of Mobile. As they say . . . stay tuned.

Dauphin Street Sound is actor Morgan Freeman's go-to recording venue when he's in town. It's also where platinum hit "You're Mines Still" by Yung Bleu was recorded. Artist Drake helped with the remix.

# ONE-STOP GLOBAL SHOP

## What's the best little deli in town?

Everyone knows the best places are the most obscure. In fact, the more obscure, the better. Located in the Spring Hill area off Old Shell Road toward West Mobile, you'll find a place that seems a little out of place next to the upscale homes. It's a little shop next to Lavretta Park called Food Pak.

Food Pak is a local staple and a serious icon for foodies. While Mobile is home to many more international shops and eateries now, Food Pak has the claim to fame of being Mobile's first. Here's the story.

In the early 1990s, Iranian immigrant Reza Hejazi found himself in a relatable predicament—he didn't have options for a job in his field of civil engineering. He took on other work before ultimately deciding to open his own business. He purchased the little shuttered grocery store off Old Shell Road and went to work.

Of course, in 1991, selling exotic flavors was trying, but the family stuck to it. They now have one of the most beloved businesses in town and sell everything from wine and beer to international sodas, 80 herbs and spices, cheeses and other dairy, grains, and a vast deli.

The deli has pita and hummus and baba ghanoush, hand-rolled stuffed grape leaves made every Friday, couscous salad,

---

In Persian, the word pak means "good quality." The freshness is in the air; the distinct aroma of international cuisine lingers pleasantly in the shop.

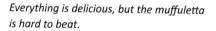

*Everything is delicious, but the muffuletta is hard to beat.*

tabouli salad, homemade feta dip, and much more. They offer Greek gyros and Italian muffulettas stuffed with a special homemade olive salad recipe that can't be beat. Everything is international at Food Pak.

Hejazi's son works with him— he started at age seven. After attending university, Mehran helps run the shop and is the artist in charge of rolling stuffed grape leaves, which frankly rarely make it out of the parking lot.

## INTERNATIONAL FOOD PAK

**What:** Mobile's oldest international food mart

**Where:** 5150 Old Shell Rd.

**Cost:** Average $10

**Pro Tip:** Take your picnic to one of the stone tables in the courtyard behind Food Pak or to Lavretta Park across the street.

# SWEET INVENTIONS, ALABAMA

## Where would we be without Mobile inventors?

They say that necessity is the mother of invention, and every marketer in today's industry can attest that the "problem/solution" model drives much of today's innovation. Then there's the happy accident, which is exactly what produced the Super Soaker.

Born in 1949, Lonnie Johnson was a curious kid. He was highly mechanical and endlessly experimental. By high school, the prodigious Johnson had invented an award-winning robot named Linex. Despite not winning first place, due to segregation still prominent in the late '60s, the scholar's primary option was the Tuskegee Institute. After college, Johnson launched a successful career at NASA.

In the early 1980s, while experimenting with ideas for a refrigeration system in his bathroom, Johnson shot a stream of water across the room and thought, "This would make a great gun." Johnson set to work and eventually created the toy water gun that blew every millennial's mind in 1991—the Super Soaker (the gun launched as the Power Drencher in 1990, but the rebranding pushed it through the roof).

Marketing really does matter. In fact, you might be intrigued to know that mobile homes came from Mobile. When the war ended in the 1940s, the population was booming; the

**BOX OWT**

**What:** Mobile's first outdoor food court (that will be made entirely of shipping containers)

**Where:** 265 Dauphin St.

**Cost:** Average $10

**Pro Tip:** Bring an umbrella, since it's an outdoor food court; Mobile's known for rain.

*A mural of famous Mobile inventors and innovators including Lonnie Johnson is painted a few block from Box Owt's Dauphin Street location.*

wool market industry, among other things, had people flocking to Mobile. People were being asked to let those homeless due to overpopulation stay in their homes.

Prichard couple James and Laura Sweet had the idea for movable prefabricated homes. The Sweet Homes did well for those who could access them. Thanks to a 1951 advertising jingle, Sweet Homes, Alabama, became the inspiration for Lynyrd Skynyrd's 1974 hit, "Sweet Home Alabama."

Finally, in 1956, Malcom McLean, a transplant to Mobile, invented shipping containers, which revolutionized the entire shipping industry and are now used around the world for shipping, storage, residences, and restaurants.

Ironically, both the hearing aid and the Klaxon (ah-oo-gah) horn are credited to Baldwin County native Miller Reese Hutchinson.

# WHODUNIT?

## Where can I solve a murder mystery on a riverboat?

They say there's been a murder on the *Perdido Queen* riverboat, and it's up to you to figure out whodunit before dessert. Lots of the folks are just like you, people who just want a good time and a good dinner, while others are actors from Bay City Improv and are along for the ride to solve the mystery.

As you set sail, the game begins. You'll need to pay attention and take notes because who knows . . . you might be a suspect! You never know who's going to be asked to step on stage and be interrogated, so it's best to be prepared.

By the end of the night and your dinner, the mystery of the *Perdido Queen* will be solved . . . as will the mystery of your hunger. Dinners are catered by Dauphin's, a casual fine-dining restaurant located on the 34th floor of the RSA Trustmark Building a few blocks from where you and yours set sail to play out your *Thin Man* detective dreams (or you can just pretend you're Tom Sawyer . . . after all, it is a riverboat).

---

### DINNER THEATER MURDER MYSTERY DINNER CRUISE

**What:** Dinner cruise and interactive murder mystery theater

**Where:** 1 S Water St.

**Cost:** $59 per person

**Pro Tip:** Murder mystery cruises run on Thursdays from 6:30–9 p.m. Regular dinner, jazz, and wine pairing cruises are other offerings during the week.

---

River platforms used to be called "widow walks" because it's where women stood watching to see if their husbands would return from crewing a riverboat.

*The* Perdido Queen *arrived to Mobile and started service in January 2019.*

Riverboats originated in England, but they were widely used in the Americas during the 1800s and the Civil War. They rose to prominence but were accident prone. Today, they're used nostalgically, which makes the dinner murder mystery a doubly fun and unique way to experience Mobile Bay.

# GLOW RIDE

## What's the best unofficial unguided pub crawl of Mobile?

If you've been around Mobile long enough, then you remember when the Loda Bier Garten was Picklefish, a primo pizza venue that had nothing to do with pickles or fish (but that had a white pizza you'd trade your mom for). The corner has always been a hub of activity and interest, and way back when it was likely a grocery or a bakery as were many corner shops.

The Loda Bier Garten, as the name *bier garten* may suggest, is a German-inspired pub with over 100 beers on tap. It embraces the convivial open-air beer garden experience with long benches and tables facing Dauphin and spilling down Joachim Street.

It's a casual gathering spot for a pint and a bite and a bike ride. The Loda Ride, which turned eight in July 2022 is Mobile's official-unofficial unguided 10-mile cycling crawl through downtown and midtown Mobile. Mid-ride, the band of beach cruisers stops at Nixon's Midtown on Old Shell and Kenneth.

Nixon's Midtown spent 80 years as Nixon's Drugs. When the current owner picked up the space, he ran with the building's existing history. Nixon's Midtown claims to "cure what ails you," and on a 10-mile bike ride around town (even at a leisurely nine miles per hour), you need a libation or two to fuel the rest of your ride.

---

**LODA BIER GARTEN**

**What:** Great place for a burger, start and end point for the Loda Ride

**Where:** 251 Dauphin St.

**Cost:** Free to ride; $3 and up for drinks and more

**Pro Tip:** The ride is BYOB (bring your own bike). Join the Facebook group Loda Ride for details on rolling in.

*Riders pause at Nixon's Midtown near Dew Drop Inn for a pint or two before heading back to the starting point, Loda Bier Garten. Photo courtesy of Greg Vrachalus*

Even though it's not a guided tour (nobody will tell you that Callaghan's used to be a meatpacking plant, for example, or where a speakeasy or a haunted house may have been), you'll still get a lot of Southern hospitality, a courtesy concert from someone's portable speakers, and a wealth of miscellaneous insider knowledge from the rascals who light up (their bike wheels) and ride. Just slide into a seat at Loda Bier Garten to learn who knows what.

The Loda Ride starts at 6:30 p.m. on Wednesdays. Riders can light up their spokes, but they also need headlights and taillights because it gets dark during the crawl.

# SOURCES

**Massacre Island**
https://alabamamoundtrail.org/mound-site/dauphin-island-shell-mound-park/
https://www.wkrg.com/haunted-history/haunted-history-of-massacre-island-alabama/
https://www.acpinfo.com/history-dauphin-island/

**The Serpents of Bienville**
https://www.al.com/live/2013/10/a_famous_mobilian_you_should_k.html
https://www.serpentsofbienville.com/blog-index/2015/9/30/bienvilles-sacred-oath
https://www.mobile.org/coupon/fort-conde-inn%3a-park-and-cruise/84/

**The Man with the Iron Hand**
https://www.southalabama.edu/org/archaeology/colonists.html
https://www.mobile.org/listing/iron-hand-brewing/1685/
https://encyclopediaofarkansas.net/entries/henri-de-tonti-2537/
https://www.britannica.com/biography/Henri-de-Tonty
*Remembering Mobile*, Caldwell Delaney, 18–24.

**Flight of the Pelican Girls**
http://www.dauphinislandhistory.com/kennedy/pelican_expand318x228.htm
https://oursouthernsouls.com/we-are-the-pelican-girls-brought-to-mobile-to-marry-french-soldiers/
https://thesaucierfamily.weebly.com/the-pelican-girls.html
https://www.al.com/living/2015/09/when_french_orphans_called_cas.html
https://apps.lib.ua.edu/blogs/coolathoole/2008/08/01/il-y-a-longtemps-the-pelican-girls-in-mobile-and-yellow-fever-comes-full-circle/

**If You Gumbo, You Gumbo**
*Old Mobile Trivia*, "Where was gumbo invented and by whom?" Malcom Steiner, 175.
https://orderonlinemenu.com/MudbugsCajunSeafood
https://mobilebaymag.com/gumbo-africans-and-creoles-on-the-gulf-coast/

**Park Place**
*Mobile! City by the Bay*, Jay Higginbottom, 142–143.
https://mobilebaymag.com/once-along-the-bay/#:~:text=In%201893%2C%20a%20massive%20storm,drum%20up%20weekend%20streetcar%20customers.
https://www.thehenryford.org/collections-and-research/digital-collections/artifact/344392/
https://www.loc.gov/item/2016806088/
https://mobilebaymag.com/bay-shell-road-c-1900/

**Pretty in Pink**
*Mobile! City by the Bay*, Jay Higginbottom, 5, 199–200, 253, 259.
*Old Mobile Trivia*, Malcom Steiner, 109, 125–126.
https://mobileazaleatrailmaids.com/our-story/
https://bellingrath.org/azaleas/
https://americanprofile.com/articles/mobile-alabama-known-as-azalea-city/

**Burn, Baby, Burn**
*Craighead's Mobile*, Caldwell Delaney, 81–83.
*Life and Confessions of the Noted Outlaw James Copeland*, Dr. J. R. S. Pitts.

**Rise Like a Phoenix**
*Craighead's Mobile*, Caldwell Delaney, 1–3.
*Mobile Ghosts: Alabama's Haunted Port City*, Elizabeth Parker, 27–31.
http://www.historymuseumofmobile.com/phoenix-fire-museum/

**A Mighty Oak**
https://www.wgpfoundation.org/historic-markers/the-boyington-oak/
https://motomom.tripod.com/BoyingtonOak
https://www.alabamabackroads.com/boyington-oak.html
https://www.wkrg.com/haunted-history/the-science-and-the-story-of-the-boyington-oak/

https://www.onlyinyourstate.com/alabama/haunted-graveyard-tree-al/

https://www.serpentsofbienville.com/blog-index/2015/10/17/boyington-oak

**Southern History Market**
https://www.loc.gov/item/al0426/

*Mobile: The New History of Alabama's First City*, Michael Thomason, 131.

https://en.wikipedia.org/wiki/Old_City_Hall_(Mobile,_Alabama)

**Stepping Back in Time**
https://www.youtube.com/watch?v=VqdzL03P3Yk

http://www.mystery411.com/Landing_oakleighhousemobile.html

https://www.al.com/live/2014/05/mystery_solved_oakleighs_cooks.html

https://www.historicoakleigh.com/

**It Was All Yellow**
http://encyclopediaofalabama.org/Article/h-1484#:~:text=He%20continued%20to%20write%20on,the%20disastrous%20epidemic%20of%201853.

https://www.mobilemedicalmuseum.org/

http://encyclopediaofalabama.org/article/h-4150

https://www.mobilemedicalmuseum.org/humanremainscollection

*Old Mobile Trivia*, Malcom Steiner, 31.

*Mobile! City by the Bay*, Jay Higginbottom, 134–135.

**Take Me to Church**
https://www.google.com/search?q=cathedral+of+the+immaculate+conception&oq=cathedral+of+the+ii512j46i20i175i199i263i512j69i57j0i12j69i60l3.4750j0j9&sourceid=chrome&ie=UTF-8

*Old Mobile Trivia*, Malcom Steiner, 78–79.

https://mobilecathedral.org/

https://mobilecathedral.org/mass

https://www.lupercaliaartsociety.com/

**Health Resort Hill**
https://greatruns.com/mobile-avenue-of-the-oaks-college-park/

https://www.al.com/life/2020/06/why-this-is-one-of-the-most-beautiful-streets-in-alabama.html

https://www.nola.com/entertainment_life/home_garden/article_2cdd3a98-2590-594f-a6ce-8fcd57666655.html

*Majestic Mobile, Mobile: The Gulf City of Alabama*, from the old catalog of Erwin Craighead, 27–45.

**Gangster's Paradise, Maybe**
https://commons.wikimedia.org/wiki/Category:Carolina_Hall

*Mobile City by the Bay*, Jay Higginbottom, 202–203.

https://newspaperarchive.com/mobile-daily-item-dec-05-1899-p-4/

http://www.loc.gov/pictures/item/al0418/

**Living History in Africatown**
*The Last Slave Ship*, Ben Raines.

https://www.latimes.com/entertainment-arts/books/story/2022-01-25/the-last-american-slave-ship-is-20-feet-underground-its-legacy-runs-far-deeper

https://www.nytimes.com/2022/01/25/books/review/the-last-slave-ship-ben-raines.html

*The Slave Ship Clotilda and the Making of AfricaTown*, USA, Natalie Robertson.

**Hoodoo You Do?**
https://lagniappemobile.com/spiritual-royalty-brings-her-magic-to-mobile/?_ga=2.83391454.913450691.1650570885-976422029.1650287853

https://conjuresouth.com/shop/

https://en.wikipedia.org/wiki/Hoodoo_(spirituality)

**Cycling through History**
https://www.adventurecycling.org/routes-and-maps/adventure-cycling-route-network/underground-railroad-ugrr/

https://www.hmdb.org/m.asp?m=102972

http://www.followthedrinkinggourd.org/What_The_Lyrics_Mean.htm

https://www.adventurecycling.org/routes-and-maps/adventure-cycling-route-network/going-digital-app-or-gpx/

https://www.southalabama.edu/libraries/mccallarchives/water_markers_sub_guide.html

https://www.npr.org/transcripts/95622632

**The Endangered Fort**

https://www.facebook.com/Fort-Gaines-Historic-Site-94521369195/?ref=page_internal

https://alabama.travel/places-to-go/historic-fort-gaines

https://www.kcbx.org/travel/2017-07-27/history-comes-alive-via-blacksmithing-reenacting-at-civil-war-era-fort-gaines-alabama

http://www.dauphinislandhistory.com/ft_gaines/fort_blksmth136expand.htm

https://www.onlyinyourstate.com/alabama/haunted-history-fort-gaines-al/

https://fort-gaines.com/

*The Story of Mobile*, Caldwell Delaney, 111–113.

**Damn the Torpedoes!**

*Mobile! City by the Bay*, Jay Higginbottom, 250–257.

https://en.m.wikipedia.org/wiki/USS_Tecumseh_(1863)

https://www.history.com/topics/american-civil-war/battle-of-mobile-bay

https://mobilebayferry.com/pricing/

**Mobile's Biggest Boom-Boom**

https://www.al.com/news/2016/05/300_alabamians_were_killed_151.html

https://hd.housedivided.dickinson.edu/node/44020

https://www.nytimes.com/1865/05/30/archives/terrible-calamity-at-mobile-explosion-of-the-rebel-ordnance-depot.html

https://en.wikipedia.org/wiki/Mobile_magazine_explosion

https://www.wisconsinhistory.org/Records/Image/IM70628

https://devastatingdisasters.com/mobile-magazine-explosion-1865/

**Oh, Deer!**

https://mobilebaymag.com/ask-mcgehee-what-is-the-history-of-mobiles-washington-square/

https://www.nytimes.com/1991/10/20/travel/history-preserved-in-mobile.html

*Hidden History of Mobile*, Joe Cuhaj, 82–84.

**The Unreconstructed Rebel**

https://mobilebaymag.com/ask-mcgehee-whats-the-history-of-the-antoinette-apartments-on-government-street/

https://www.findagrave.com/memorial/30565410/augusta-jane-wilson

*Hidden History of Mobile*, Joe Cuhaj, 69–75.

**Joe Cain and the People's Walking Parade**

http://www.mobilemask.com/

http://www.mobilemask.com/joe-cain.html

https://www.facebook.com/JoeCainParadingSociety/

https://www.facebook.com/JoeCainFootmarchers/

Personal experience (participant).

**Making Widows Merry**

https://www.mobile.org/events/mardi-gras/joe-cain-day/

http://www.mobilemask.com/joe-cain.html

**Exploring New Traditions**

https://www.facebook.com/conde.explorers/about/?ref=page_internal

http://www.mobilemask.com/conde-explorers.html

https://blackamericaweb.com/2014/03/03/little-known-black-history-fact-origins-of-mardi-gras/

https://www.jacobinmag.com/2022/02/segregated-mardi-grass-carnival-parade-mobile-alabama#:~:text=Decades%20after%20the%20end%20of,still%20maintain%20white%2Donly%20membership.

**Oh Baby Cakes (The Next One's on You)**

https://www.southernliving.com/holidays-occasions/mardi-gras/king-cake-meaning

https://www.kingcakeoff.com/

http://templedowntown.com/origins.php

**MoonPie over Mobile**

https://www.southernkitchen.com/story/entertain/2021/07/24/mobiles-mardi-gras-moonpie-cake-tradition/8083805002/

**And the Beat Goes On**

https://www.classy.org/event/2022-king-cake-off/e356005

https://randazzokingcake.com/history

https://www.eater.com/22268353/king-cake-history-tradition-mardi-gras

https://www.facebook.com/LighthouseBakery/

**All That Jazz**

https://en.wikipedia.org/wiki/James_Reese_Europe

https://www.loc.gov/item/ihas.200038842/

https://www.britannica.com/biography/James-Reese-Europe

https://mobilebaymag.com/tastings-kazoola-eatery-entertainment/

**Prohibited Port City Imports**

https://mobilebaymag.com/mobile-spirits/

*Conversation with Chuck Torries*, April 2022.

*A Thousand Thirsty Beaches*, Lisa Lindquist Dorr.

*Mobile! City by the Bay*, Jay Higginbottom, 164–176.

https://npgallery.nps.gov/GetAsset/89d9e8bd-081f-44d7-bd1f-6c76ccb5bfb3

**Walk Softly, Speakeasy**

https://mobilebaymag.com/mobile-spirits/

*Conversation with Chuck Torries*, April 2022.

*A Thousand Thirsty Beaches*, Lisa Lindquist Dorr.

https://www.secrethistorytours.com/tour/r/

Participation at speakeasy tour premier at Alchemy Tavern with Todd Duren, July 2019.

**The Malaga Inn**

https://www.instagram.com/p/CDZ0vNwj2Sc/

http://www.awhf.org/levert.html

http://encyclopediaofalabama.org/article/h-2355

https://www.al.com/life/2020/04/the-alabama-inn-built-atop-a-secret-tunnel.html

https://www.onlyinyourstate.com/alabama/haunting-story-of-al-hotel/

https://www.youtube.com/watch?v=4-snW4vEWQY

https://www.youtube.com/watch?v=-BF2KVsQIcg

**Right up Automotive Alley**

https://mobilebaymag.com/the-resurgence-of-automobile-alley/

https://www.thecheesecottagellc.com/

https://www.facebook.com/greersstlouismarket/

**Swinging for the Fences**

http://encyclopediaofalabama.org/article/h-1572

http://encyclopediaofalabama.org/article/h-4122

*Old Mobile Trivia*, Malcom Steiner, 35, 37, 106–107, 152, 155.

**The Battle House Bride**

Interview with in-house historian for Visit South in 2014.

Secret History Tour with Todd Duren, March 29, 2019.

**Haunted House in De Tonti**

*Mobile Ghosts: Alabama's Haunted Port City*, Elizabeth Parker, 39–45.

https://www.al.com/realestate-news/2017/11/cool_spaces_a_breath_of_fresh.html

https://mobilebaymag.com/return-to-de-tonti/

https://en.wikipedia.org/wiki/De_Tonti_Square_Historic_District

**Pirate's Honey**

https://mobilebaymag.com/the-history-of-pirates-cove/#:~:text=The%20name%20Pirates%20Cove%20has,of%20Perdido%20Pass%20and%20survive.

https://www.theatlantic.com/magazine/archive/1872/07/why-semmes-of-the-alabama-was-not-tried-part-i/520365/

https://www.theatlantic.com/magazine/archive/1872/08/why-semmes-of-the-alabama-was-not-tried-part-ii/520371/

https://www.theadmiralhotel.com/press

https://en.wikipedia.org/wiki/Raphael_Semmes

https://mobilebaymag.com/the-history-of-pirates-cove/#:~:text=The%20name%20Pirates%20Cove%20has,of%20Perdido%20Pass%20and%20survive.

https://en.wikipedia.org/wiki/Admiral_Hotel_(Mobile,_Alabama)

https://www.theadmiralhotel.com/about

**Taste of Heaven**
https://www.al.com/life/2018/12/mobiles-visitation-shop-is-home-to-all-things-heavenly.html

https://cloisteredlife.com/directory/mobile

https://mobilebaymag.com/on-prayer-and-chocolate/

**It's Good to Be Greek**
https://greekfestmobile.com/

https://mobilebaymag.com/the-greek-legacy/

Conversation with Charles "Chuck" Torrey, Living History Curator, History Museum of Mobile, April 2022.

https://3georges.com/

https://www.al.com/living/2018/03/three_georges_the_little_candy.html#:~:text=The%20century%2Dold%20Three%20Georges,owners%20to%20make%20their%20confections.

**Middle Bay Moo House**
https://www.lighthousefriends.com/light.asp?ID=650

https://ahc.alabama.gov/properties/middlebay/middlebay.aspx

https://en.wikipedia.org/wiki/Middle_Bay_Light

https://953thebear.com/middle-bay-lighthouse-strange-alabama/

https://yellowhammernews.com/learn-the-history-behind-alabamas-136-year-old-middle-bay-lighthouse/

https://www.weather.gov/mob/1916Hurricane#:~:text=July%205th%20Hurricane%20of%201916&text=The%20maximum%20winds%20at%20landfall,measured%20on%20Fort%20Morgan%2C%20AL.

https://www.al.com/living/2016/07/vintage_1916_photos_show_when.html

**The Hermit of Goat Island**
*Mobile! City by the Bay*, Jay Higginbottom, 241–242.

**Plane Crazy**
https://mobilebaymag.com/the-aviators/

Interview with Chuck Torries, History Museum of Mobile, April 2022.

**The Mighty A**
https://www.ussalabama.com/explore/uss-alabama-battleship/

http://encyclopediaofalabama.org/article/h-2958

https://coast360.com/coastal-stories/uss-alabama/

https://www.history.navy.mil/our-collections/photography/us-navy-ships/battleships/alabama-bb-60.html

**The Cannon**
*Old Mobile Trivia*, Malcom Steiner, 53, 55.

https://www.al.com/entertainment/2015/01/mobile_mardi_gras_101_a_primer.html#:~:text=Mobile's%20Mardi%20Gras%20colors%20are,and%20the%20green%20for%20faith.

https://www.hmdb.org/m.asp?m=149322

**Flower Power**
https://bellingrath.org/azaleas/

Personal interviews. (The author is the great niece of the late Doc Brown, who managed Bellingrath in the 1970s. He and his wife lived on the property. The author's father, Joe Brown, spent his formative years assisting in gardening while his uncle served as manager.)

https://bellingrath.org/remembering-doc-brown-bellingrath/

https://bellingrath.org/bellingrath-blog-fooling-mother-nature/#:~:text=Rather%20than%20planting%20tulips%20in,at%20temperatures%20around%2035%20degrees.

https://www.gardenvisit.com/gardens/bellingrath_gardens

**21st-Century Theater**
https://mobilebaymag.com/bygone-structures/

https://mobilebaymag.com/empire-theatre-1940/

http://cinematreasures.org/theaters/42115

http://cinematreasures.org/theaters/56384

*Old Mobile Trivia*, Malcom Steiner, 129.

http://crescenttheater.pythonanywhere.com/#about

**The Show Must Go On**

https://www.asmglobal.com/p/our-portfolio/theaters/saenger-theater-mobile#:~:text=TheatersSaenger%20Theater%20%2D%20Mobile&text=When%20Mobile's%20Saenger%20Theatre%20opened,in%20Cuba%20and%20Puerto%20Rico.

https://en.wikipedia.org/wiki/Saenger_Theatre_(Mobile,_Alabama)

https://www.asmglobalmobile.com/saenger-theatre/history-of-the-saenger-theatre

https://mobilebaymag.com/ask-mcgehee-didnt-mobiles-saenger-theatre-originally-have-a-pipe-organ/

**Meal Fit for a King**

*Hidden History of Mobile*, Joe Cuhaj, 146–150.

https://mobilebaymag.com/elvis-the-early-years/

https://www.roadsideamerica.com/tip/17268

https://www.nytimes.com/2003/07/27/travel/elvis-slept-here-gators-sleep-there.html

http://jimmyjoemeeker.blogspot.com/2009/03/elvis-once-slept-here-wmob-1360-am.html

**Cookie-Cutter Home**

https://www.hmdb.org/m.asp?m=149317

https://www.kateshepardhouse.com/blog.htm

https://www.kateshepardhouse.com/history.htm

https://www.onlyinyourstate.com/alabama/haunted-bed-and-breakfast-al/

https://www.findagrave.com/memorial/103179482/kate-shepard

https://www.eastbaytimes.com/2007/12/09/historic-alabama-bb-has-story-to-tell/

**Cheeseburger in Paradise**

*Old Mobile Trivia*, Malcom Steiner, 69.

http://encyclopediaofalabama.org/article/h-1219#:~:text=Singer%20and%20songwriter%20Jimmy%20Buffett,themes%20in%20his%20artistic%20output.

https://www.mobile.org/things-to-do/history/colorful-characters/

**Renaissance Man**

*The Happy Table of Eugene Walter*, Donald Goodman and Thomas Head.

https://mobilebaymag.com/when-eugene-wrote-for-us-memories-of-the-80s/

https://en.wikipedia.org/wiki/Eugene_Walter

http://encyclopediaofalabama.org/Article/h-2557

https://journal.alabamachanin.com/2015/09/eugene-walter-mobiles-renaissance-man/

**The Haunted Book Shop**

Interviews with Angela Trigg, Summer 2019, April 2022.

Interview with Mr. Bingley, April 2022.

**The Bakery**

https://www.redorwhitewine.com/mobile-location

Smith's Bakery Mobile 1950s Clark-Shaw Magnet School Oral Histories of Alabama (https://www.youtube.com/watch?v=Syev8qFTvXs)

Interview with owner at (current) Nixon Drugs, c. 2007.

https://mobilebaymag.com/tastings-red-or-white-wine-gourmet-center/

https://www.bakingbusiness.com/articles/50493-gordon-smith-unified-the-commercial-baking-industry#:~:text=Smith%20arrived%20in%20Mobile%20from,1900%20and%20launched%20Smith's%20Bakeries.

https://mobilebaymag.com/restaurant-review-nixons/

https://books.google.com/books?id=xtNfAAAAIAAJ&pg=PA6598&lpg=PA6598&dq=1108+dauphin+street+part+of+the+bakery?&source=bl&ots=lg92kY5Q0y&sig=ACfU3U0B

ufS4XL81lsa76OVHYc8go7shIw&hl=
en&sa=X&ved=2ahUKEwiyzZ_
x1Jf3AhUhRDABHfYjCh0Q6AF6BAgDEA
M#v=onepage&q=1108%20dauphin%20
street%20part%20of%20the%20
bakery%3F&f=false

**Ice, Ice, Baby**
https://lagniappemobile.com/114-year-
old-crystal-ice-company-changing-hands/
https://mobilebaymag.com/review-the-
ice-box-bar/
https://books.google.com/books?id
=8z0AAAAAMAAJ&pg=PA124&lpg
=PA124&dq=cost+of+ice+in+mobile
+1900s&source=bl&ots=475Km
GZBtP&sig=ACfU3U3vJ_SMAXTj8Fky
zNS292Lxly3zJQ&hl=en&sa=X&ved=
2ahUKEwicqe-ahrf3AhXammoFHQ-
eCy8Q6AF6BAgoEAM
https://www.theiceboxbar.com/

**Dig into the Garage**
https://houston.eater.
com/2017/4/6/15197940/sucking-
crawfish-heads-yes-or-no
https://www.thegaragemobile.
com/?fbclid=IwAR2iUkrWvoxt23zTNBh
rxd2MCaSiDAvYVkx2ENTbvkfbx9zb6Y6
e23HM5v0
https://www.facebook.com/
thegaragemobile/

**Curious Coffee Culture**
https://www.thesocialexp.com/
knucklebones-elixir-co
https://www.thesocialexp.com/
Interview with barista (February 2022).
https://www.serdas.com/our-story/

**Follow the Oyster Trail**
https://oystergardening.org/the-oyster-
trail/
https://www.facebook.com/
TheOysterTrail/
http://www.downtownmobile.org/
uploads/pdf/oyster_trail_map.pdf

**West Indies Salad**
https://eatalabamaseafood.com/articles/
story/west-indies-salad-bayleys-seafood-
restaurant
https://www.atlasobscura.com/foods/
west-indies-salad

**Jubilee by the Sea**
https://www.wsfa.com/2020/09/09/
something-that-only-happens-two-places-
world-just-occurred-mobile-bay/
https://en.wikipedia.org/wiki/Mobile_Bay_
jubilee
https://www.wsfa.com/2020/09/09/
something-that-only-happens-two-places-
world-just-occurred-mobile-bay/
https://historydaily.org/jubilee-mobile-
bays-unique-ocean-phenomenon-equals-
good-eating
https://www.wkrg.com/baldwin-county/
small-jubilee-sighting-off-fairhope-pier/

**America's Amazon**
*Saving America's Amazon*, Ben Raines.
Personal experience (kayaking to
Champion Cypress / Indian Mounds in
Jessamine Bayou).

**Blessing of the Fleet**
https://stmargaretbayoulabatre.org/
history
https://www.smarthomeamerica.
org/assets/catalog/Bayou-La-Batre-
Comprehensive-Plan-2018.pdf
https://www.facebook.com/
FleetBlessingBayouLaBatre/

**Pretty Fly Place**
https://www.dauphinislandbirds.
com/_files/ugd/0759d0_
c98fe0ed73d043b2bdcb300f7f0c7e6e.pdf
https://www.dauphinislandbirds.com/al-
coastal-birding-trail
https://alabamabirdingtrails.com/trails/
coastal/
https://www.dauphinislandbirds.com/
https://mynbc15.com/news/local/
the-new-plan-for-mobile-bay-raises-
environmental-concerns-for-local-officials

**We Are the Rainiest?**
https://worldpopulationreview.com/us-
city-rankings/rainiest-cities-in-the-us
Personal experience.

**See You Later, Alligator!**
https://www.nwf.org/Educational-
Resources/Wildlife-Guide/Reptiles/
American-Alligator#:~:text=American%20
alligators%20are%20large%20

crocodilians,larger%20than%20females%20on%20average.

https://www.airboatadventures.net/

**Estuarium Deep Dive**
https://www.disl.edu/aquarium
https://www.disl.edu/dhp/family-camp
https://www.disl.edu/aquarium/adventures-tours-and-talks

**Doggie Paddle**
https://www.facebook.com/groups/440154882824956/
Personal experience.

**Hip, Hip Hippie Beach**
Personal Experience.
Word of mouth.
https://www.al.com/life/2021/03/mobiles-hippie-beach-is-going-up-for-sale.html

**Sup, Y'all?**
https://purealohaadventures.com/alabama/
https://purealohaadventures.com/alabama/stand-up-paddle-board-lesson-tour/
Personal experience.

**Game, Set, Match**
https://www.mobiletenniscenter.net/
https://www.facebook.com/mobiletenniscenter
https://en.wikipedia.org/wiki/Langan_(Municipal)_Park
https://www.al.com/sports/2011/09/davis_cup_tennis_stars_mardy_f.html
http://serveitupwithlove.com/

**Vaulting about Town**
https://www.facebook.com/Dauphinstreetvault
https://www.dauphinstreetvault.org/
https://www.mobilesportsauthority.com/2022-dauphin-street-vault
https://www.ciscoathletic.com/blog/interesting-facts-about-pole-vaulting/

**Urban Wilderness**
https://www.redbeardsoutfitter.com/glenn-sebastian-nature-trail/
https://www.southalabama.edu/departments/campusrec/facilityrental/naturetrail.html

https://www.alltrails.com/trail/us/alabama/glenn-sebastian-nature-trail-white-route
https://rootsrated.com/stories/a-quick-dirty-guide-to-south-alabama-s-best-mountain-biking

**Secret Garden City**
https://www.youtube.com/watch?v=ZmeEIX7dRco
https://www.al.com/realestate-news/2017/11/cool_spaces_a_breath_of_fresh.html
https://cornerstonegarden.org/
https://www.thisisalabama.org/2018/11/06/a-treasure-of-a-garden-is-hidden-in-plain-sight-along-mobiles-busy-government-street/5vqexyopqra53clzmyfonyn73e/
https://www.onlyinyourstate.com/alabama/passport-japanese-garden-al/
https://southserves.southalabama.edu/agency/detail/?agency_id=93056
https://mobilejapanesegarden.com/index.htm

**Pirate's Pool**
https://www.facebook.com/PiratesBarandGrill/
https://www.acpinfo.com/pirates-bar-and-grill-on-dauphin-island/
https://www.piratesbarandgrill.com/menus
https://www.pirateglossary.com/namecalling

**The Crichton Leprechaun**
https://www.youtube.com/watch?v=5vi35H9H4Og
https://www.wheredagoldat.com/
https://www.callaghansirishsocialclub.com/

**That's Just Nuts**
https://www.cityofmobile.org/city-updates/city-of-mobile-to-begin-relocating-some-squirrels-from-bienville-square/
https://www.al.com/news/2022/01/overpopulated-and-causing-damage-mobile-to-relocate-some-squirrels-from-historic-park.html
https://mobilearts.org/mysticsobs/
https://lagniappemobile.com/things-getting-bit-squirrely-around/

**Film, Forrest, Film**
Interview with Winston Groom for Lagniappe cover story on Alabama's film initiative, 2009.

https://www.imdb.com/search/title/?locations=Mobile%2C+Alabama%2C+USA

https://www.themobilerundown.com/movies-filmed-in-alabama/

https://www.cityofmobile.org/departments/mobile-film-office/

Conversation with Haunted Book Shop owner Angela Trigg.

https://mynbc15.com/news/local/heres-what-the-new-nicolas-cage-movie-being-shot-in-mobile-is-about

https://mobilebaymag.com/mobile-in-the-movies/

**See Art, Walk**
https://mobilearts.org/art-walk/

https://www.al.com/life/2022/01/food-networks-raid-the-fridge-to-feature-mobile-chef-erica-barrett.html

**Folks Bond at the Pond**
https://www.facebook.com/FrogPond.BlueMoonFarms/about/?ref=page_internal

http://thepokearound.com/2016/02/25/the-frog-pond-experience-a-hidden-gem-of-the-south/#:~:text=Modeled%20after%20Levon%20Helm's%20Midnight,%2425%20or%20%2430%20donation%20each.

https://folk.org/

https://www.thefrogpondatbluemoonfarm.com/about/

**Cedar Street Social Club**
http://www.dauphinstreetsound.com/

https://mobilebaymag.com/jake-peavys-second-act/

https://bleacherreport.com/articles/2756799-i-need-a-miracle-every-day-jake-peavy-picks-up-pieces-of-a-shattered-life

https://restaurantjump.com/cedar-street-social-club-36602/

https://www.facebook.com/theinsiderfoodhall/

https://lagniappemobile.com/developers-plan-mobiles-first-food-hall/

**One-Stop Global Shop**
https://www.al.com/news/mobile/2014/07/american_dreamers_meet_four_su.html#:~:text=Food%20Pak%20founder%20Reza%20Hejazi,was%20just%206%20years%20old.

https://mobilebaymag.com/25-food-innovators-you-should-know/

**Sweet Inventions, Alabama**
https://www.biography.com/news/lonnie-johnson-invent-super-soaker

https://mobilebaymag.com/eureka/

https://www.facebook.com/Boxowt

**Whodunit?**
https://www.facebook.com/mobilewaterfront/about/?ref=page_internal

https://perdidoqueen.com/murder-mystery-dinner-theater-cruise-mobile-al-perdido-queen/

https://ancestralfindings.com/how-riverboats-and-steamers-shaped-american-history/

**Glow Ride**
https://www.facebook.com/groups/719871091486454

https://lodabeer.com/

https://mobilebaymag.com/restaurant-directory/loda-bier-garten/

# INDEX